EXPERT ADVICE
ON HOW TO
CULTIVATE YOUR CAREER

Marya Triandafellos

Print ISBN: ISBN-13: 978-0-9979654-7-6
E book ISBN: ISBN-13: 978-0-9979654-8-3

Library of Congress Control Number: 2018938409

Printed and Bound in the USA
First Printing May 2018

Published by Simply Good Press
Montclair, New Jersey 07043
simplygoodpress.com

Cover Graphics: Philippe Nicolas

Visit: CareerX.co

This book is dedicated to my parents, Irene and James Triandafellos, who instilled in me the value of education and supported me in my determination to cultivate my unique career path.

For my Mom, your dream was to write a book, but you never did. I was compelled to carry out your dream—inspired by your incessant positivity and belief in me.

For my Dad, I remember you struggling as you studied for your GED while you were an executive at a banking institution. You taught me that you can learn what you need by listening, watching, and doing—the method I've used for almost everything I know today.

 A big thank you to my cheerleaders and expert team! Without you I couldn't have made it!

1 Lena Rodriguez
2 Jane Tabatchnick
3 Kelin Rapp
4 Lisa Goldman
5 Michelle Hanggi
6 Michael Triandafellos

To my contributors, many thanks for your expertise, insights, and story sharing!

1 Cindy Schwartz, Director of Talent & Knowledge at the Anti-Defamation League
2 Rachel Garrett, Career and Leadership Coach, rachel-garrett.com
3 Annie Lawler, breathingspacetherapies.com
4 Jeremy Bieger, Co-founder & CEO of Pulse Insights, pulseinsights.com, jbieger@pulseinsights.com
5 Luke Haseloff, Business Development Director, Digital Operative, digitaloperative.com, twitter.com/lukehaseloff
6 Cathleen Rybak, LCSW R, 24 Davis Avenue, Poughkeepsie NY 12528
7 Josh Bresnick
8 Kathy Marryat, Marketing Executive and Non-Profit Volunteer
9 Nancy M. Stuart, Ph.D., Dean, Hartford Art School, University of Hartford, hartford.edu/art

Contents

Frequently Asked Questions

Introduction

What does the title "Career X" mean?

The X in "Career X" has multiple meanings. The X stands for a variable used an algebra equation, that represents an unknown entity. Although many of us will have a career, we don't always know exactly how it will unfold, the significance of what we are doing in the moment, or what we will do next. The X represents that uncertainty, but also excitement and potential! Similar to the process of solving an algebra equation, start with what you know and progress step-by-step until you reach a solution.

The symbolic, unknown value of X also means you can make that X whatever you want it to be: Career as a Business Executive, Career Musician, Career Explorer, Career Helping People. That is the essence of this book: providing guidance on how to define X—which is fluid and contextual, and, once defined, how to cultivate your career to achieve X.

Who is this book for?

Most people looking to follow a conventional path of working for a startup, small business, or corporation will find value in this book. However, it is geared towards high school and college students, recent grads launching their career or professionals who want to change their career. Each of these situations is a turning point—which can be challenging—but made easier with support from others who have been through similar experiences.

If you are in high school or college and wondering what it takes to launch and create a career that is meaningful to you, this book can guide, direct, and hopefully, inspire you. If you are pivoting to a new job or career, or have been out of the job market for some time, this book will inform you of current best practices.

Why is this book different?

From my conversations with students, I learned that most wonder what they will encounter when they graduate. Although career centers, online blogs, and career sites provide many bytes of info, there aren't resources that cover the full spectrum of the career life cycle and how it is intertwined with life in the way I present it here. Career X outlines a broad, multi-disciplinary approach to defining, cultivating, and succeeding in your career—and by extension, in your life.

Why do you need it?

First, don't feel bad about not knowing this info. How to cultivate your career is not taught in college courses, but it's expected that you'll assemble this information in a piecemeal fashion. That's no easy task because today's careers are not linear, as they were a generation or two ago. Careers are complex and unpredictable. You may work several jobs at once, experience multiple job types—such as gig worker and full-timer—and pursue several different careers in your lifetime. It is essential that you learn how to actively cultivate your own career from a 360-degree perspective!

After reading this book (which provides a broad, high-level view of the career life cycle), you can assess your knowledge gaps and decide what topics you'd like to research further.

What is the inspiration and the goal?

Friends have asked me to provide career advice to recent graduates looking for jobs in digital, design, and tech. Through these informal conversations, I heard the questions of high school students deciding on colleges and college grads grappling with how to find their first job.

I noticed a huge knowledge gap for graduates transitioning from college to the professional world. Most graduates get little support about the nuanced requirements are for landing a job in various professions.

Rather, it seems, most institutes of higher learning primarily deliver best practices for the essentials of a job search: how to write a resume or answer interview questions. The quality of this information is uneven—some schools are good at it, others are not.

My goal is to fill the gap between graduation and your first job, between one career and your next. I'll provide a roadmap of what to expect in the journey. Going into a situation blind makes it more difficult. If you create a career vision, it will help you picture the future. Your vision will help you move forward into the unknown with confidence, purpose, and be better prepared to respond to unexpected circumstances—good and bad.

We are all drawn to people who exude confidence and purpose. As a great example, watch woman's education advocate and the youngest Nobel Prize laureate Malala Yousafzai speak. She is so confident of her life's purpose; it is infectious and demands our attention and respect.

My goal is to inspire you to do the hard work of finding your life's purpose, and help you to be successful in your search for meaning. We can never be in control of everything that impacts us, but with intentionality, we can be the force that drives our life experiences.

Who am I?

What credentials do I have to write this book? By trade, I am not a Human Resources professional, recruiter, or educator. I am an entrepreneur, design management consultant, designer, visual artist, and now, author :)

I've culled my personal experiences finding jobs, serving hundreds of clients, and hiring for my own design businesses and for creative teams at Fortune 100 corporations. To supplement my knowledge and experience, I've invited subject matter experts to contribute their know-how, and I've conducted extensive research on the key topics in the book.

How is this book structured?

As your guide, this book provides an overview of the requirements for a successful career. The process starts by defining what a career is, and then continues through the career life cycles—all the steps of finding and succeeding in a job. Designed to be to easily digested, it's organized into four parts:

1. What is a Career?
2. How Do I Cultivate My Career?
3. The Job Search Life Cycle
4. Your Job Search Toolkit

Each part contains frequently asked questions (FAQs) that are sequentially numbered. Use it as a reference book—find a question in the list of Frequently Asked Questions and jump to the answer—or read it sequentially from cover to cover. Following are some highlights.

"What is a Career?" starts with key definitions, and then moves on to exploring the big questions usually asked about jobs, careers, and purpose, such as "How can I make money from something I love?" and "How do I know if a job is right for me?" In "Employment Structures Overview," the three main categories of employment are defined along with their key characteristics. Although this book is focused on landing a job as an employee, we touch on the positions of contingent worker and business owner/entrepreneur. As the job market stands today, it's likely you'll experience all three at some point in your career. For example, you might take on freelance assignments to keep employed between full time jobs.

Next, we discuss career stories—narratives of the career experiences of recent graduates and mid-career professionals. These are meant to trigger your imagination and help you envision or reinvent your career story. Everyone has a unique path, but after hearing many career stories, I distinguished a handful of archetypes. Some people stay with one company in the same role for their entire career and love it. Others make dramatic changes to seemingly unrelated jobs. Listening to the stories of others gives us the faith to believe anything is possible!

"How do I cultivate my career?" progresses from an inward to an outward focus. In the sections regarding "Self-Awareness," learn who you are and find your purpose through a feedback loop of continual exploration.

Self-awareness means deeply understanding all the dimensions of your being—appearance, preferences, behaviors, achievements, and skills—and culminates in building your professional brand. Your success starts with knowing what you're good at, what you like, and how you can incorporate learnings from your experiences into your personal brand.

Armed with self-awareness, the "Network & Relationships Overview," details how to venture out and engage with others. Discover how to initiate and build relationships with a variety of people who can guide you and who you can mentor. No one gets ahead without help from other people! You can start building reciprocal relationship right now: in your classroom, with extended family, with neighbors, on athletic teams, or in clubs. Build your network by being supportive and asking for support when you need it.

Next is the "Intelligence Gathering Overview," which describes how to find fact-based information about jobs, companies, industries, and global trends through research, training, interviewing, and attending events. This may sound a little "CIA," but it takes diligence to acquire the truth. Included is a summary of the predominant trends influencing today's job market and what radical changes to expect in the near future.

Once you've defined your ideal job, start the step-by-step process of finding a job in "The Job Search Life Cycle." This covers the process of looking for and finding a full-time job. You'll learn how to find job openings, what questions can and can't be asked in an interview, and how to get promoted, to name a few FAQs.

We don't stop there! Once you've landed a job, how do you achieve "Success in Your Role?" Although this could be a book on its own, critical FAQs—such as "How can I optimize my relationship with a manager?," "What makes a great leader?," and "How can I get promoted?"—are featured.

At some point, you will start the cycle again as described in "Transitioning to Your Next Job Overview." Here, we provide a brief overview of how to know when it's time to leave and how to gracefully exit your current job.

We end with current best practices for the tools you need to launch and evolve your career—your resume, LinkedIn profile, and business card.

Thank you for trusting me! I wish you success in your endeavors. Be patient with yourself, and you can travel through your career and enjoy the journey. Angela Lee Duckworth provides inspiration in her book, *Grit*. She determined that "[g]rit is passion and perseverance for very long-term goals..." and "is living life like it's a marathon, not a sprint."[1] It's time to get your grit on and cultivate your career! Onward to our marathon!

What is a Career?

1
What is a job?

Let's start with the dictionary definition of "job." The Merriam-Webster dictionary cites four entries, two of which are relevant:

> **JOB**: (3b) a specific duty, role, or function
> (3c) a regular remunerative position[2]

Practically speaking, a job is a regular set of functions you perform for which you receive financial compensation. A job is a transaction whereby you execute agreed upon tasks in exchange for an income.

It is more than that, however. It is where you will spend much of your day and most your life. Beyond a transaction, your job:

- Contributes to your social status
- Affects how you feel about yourself
- Impacts your success
- Influences which people will be in your network
- Defines the course of your career

When you think of what job you want, consider both the practical, income earning dimensions, and the less tangible, less predictable dimensions that will impact your life. A job is an opportunity for you to show what you can do, to help others, and to grow.

2
What is a career?

If a job is what you do to earn an income, then what is a career? Let's review the official definition:

> **CAREER**: A field for, or pursuit of, consecutive progressive achievement, especially in public, professional, or business life[3]

The "consecutive progressive achievement" happens as, over time and through multiple jobs, you improve your skills, grow in experience, and hone your expertise. Although most of your career progress will happen on the job, the success of your career is also evaluated based on your philanthropic contributions and your expressions of leadership. In other words, your career is more than your achievements; it is your achievements in the context of your behaviors and your reputation in the world.

Recently, we've seen an example of the importance of behavior and reputation with the "me too" movement: women speaking out about sexual violence and harassment. Some of the accused men have built amazing success with wealth, awards, and recognition, but their improper/ illegal treatment of women and co-workers has crushed their careers and their lives.

What is today's career experience?

In today's marketplace, unlike the world of your parents or grandparents, it is highly unlikely that you'll work for one company for the entirety of your career. By the time you are 35, you'll probably have worked in 10-14 jobs. Since the average job takes 1.5-2.5 months to find, that means you'll spend at least one (and up to three) solid years looking for a job by the time you're 35.

"Gone is the era of the lifetime career, let alone the life-long job and the economic security that came with it, having been replaced by a new economy intent on recasting full-time employees into contractors, vendors and temporary workers," although the US jobs statistics haven't yet caught up with this transformation.[4]

When does my career start?

You will have a unique career path, defined by what ideas and plans you develop and the decisions you make. It could start, as it did for musician Justin Bieber, at two years old, when his family posted a video on YouTube of him hand-drumming a sophisticated beat, or your career could start later in life as it did for Julia Child, whose TV cooking show revolutionized cooking in the U.S when she was 50. Her career was previously in advertising.

Your career may start when serendipity strikes and you meet someone influential during your daily routine. Toni Braxton, Grammy-winning recording artist, caught her big break at a gas station. She was singing to herself and pumping gas when a record producer overheard her and asked Braxton to record a demo at his studio.[5]

For most people, careers start upon graduation from high school, vocational school, or college, but don't worry if it takes time to figure out what you want to do. You are certainly not alone. Reading this book is a good start!

3
What's the difference between a "job" and a "career?"

A "job" is a subset of a "career." Together, jobs can become the building blocks of a career, but without career cultivation, you'll go from job to job without a destination. Jobs that advance your objectives contribute to your career.

Building your career is a multifaceted process that progresses from the inside out: from a comprehension of yourself to understanding how you fit in the context of the world and how you can make the best contribution possible.

Not every job in your lifetime will contribute towards your career progression. Sometimes a job will trigger an advancement in your career, but other times, it may solely provide income. For example, if you decide to change careers, but need education to do so, you might work a job that doesn't interest you just to earn income while attending school.

Before you start looking for a job, understand what you need from that job. Is this a "income only" job, or will you learn something that is currently missing from your tool box? For example, in my career, I realized I needed to learn more about large digital platforms and marketing large-scale e-commerce experiences, so I closed my business and took a full-time job in a corporation with millions of customers.

4
What is career cultivation?

Career cultivation, is my take on what is commonly called career management. Career "management" is a misnomer. It means that something exists and you are supervising it. Cultivation, on the other hand, means to "foster the growth of" which better describes how to achieve the goal of a successful career.[6] A successful career—successful by your own definition—should be a synthesis of what you value in life and what you do for a living. Cultivating your career means YOU foster its growth, not your employer, your career counselor, or your relatives.

Career cultivation doesn't mean that when you graduate from college you'll know what you'll be doing for the next 40 years! It means that you consciously plan, set goals, assess, and modify your path as your situation evolves. Just as you would cultivate a garden, start from small seeds of ideas or interests, and nourish them until they flourish.

Career Considerations

Especially when starting out, you will have many questions about your career, particularly how to make it fit into your lifestyle and allow you to be who you are. We will answer a few of these broader questions, such as how to make money from something you love, and how to assess if a job is right for you.

5
Where will my career take me?

Annie Lawler, of Breathing Space Therapies in London answers this FAQ:

> The answer is simple. Anywhere you want to go. The important thing is to love what you do, so that you can put your heart into it. You don't have to fit into someone else's idea of what you should be doing. There may be times when you rethink what you are doing and turn back or even change your route completely. Some of these decisions may be totally yours or may be enforced. It doesn't matter. In my experience, nothing is wasted. Your skills can often be used in ways you never expected, but which can be exciting. The most important thing with careers, as with life in general, is to follow your heart wherever it leads. It sounds trite, but it works. Life's too short and too precious to settle for drudgery.[7]

6
What is my dream?

Your dream is a vision, an imagined future of your very best, superstar self! What would bring you fulfillment? What could your biggest contribution to the world be? How could you build a legacy?

Not everyone formulates their dream during the same stage of life. Your dream may come to you as a very young person or when you're older. It may appear to you like a bolt of lightning, or you may struggle to determine what it is. It may require learning parts of many disparate fields. It may morph over time.

Your dream starts with a realization, a feeling, an experience which can then be further honed by writing it down and planning what steps it will take to achieve it.

Your dream can be a specific job, such as the CMO of a specific company, or it can be a desired lifestyle, such as only working from home a few hours a week or traveling the world as a journalist. Whatever it is, it must start with a written statement to bring it into the physical world.

Alain de Botton presented a TED talk in which he concluded that while society tells you that you can do anything, the reality is that it's up to you to realistically decide your boundaries. We are made to feel that if we strive to be a cultural icon, then we can experience the success of a billionaire like Bill Gates, but the likelihood of that happening is about the same as that of a peasant becoming a French aristocrat in the time of Marie Antoinette!

However, that doesn't mean that you can't be successful or have an impact on the world. First, strive to be the master of your own ambition by knowing yourself. Use each moment to build on what you do best.

The Five W's

An exercise to help craft your dream statement is to write your answers to the following "Five W" questions.

1 **WHO**—The people, company, or entity that will benefit from the realization of your dream.
2 **WHAT**—The definition of your expertise: the skills, passion, experience, and knowledge you've acquired that will help you perform a set of behaviors that is of value to others (the "who").
3 **WHERE**—The location in which the "what" will take place, ranging from an office to a factory to a village in another country.
4 **WHEN**—What are the circumstances that trigger the need for your expertise? Is it a routine occurrence or an emergency? Is it triggered at a specific time of day, time of year, or because of an event like a financial crisis or an earthquake?
5 **WHY**—What reasons make your expertise valuable in the world? What greater purpose does it serve?

Check back periodically, and review what you wrote. Answer the questions again. Has anything changed? Are you refining your initial responses, or have you made a drastic change? Keep track of changes over the course of your career.

7

How do my personal life experiences affect my career?

Specific experiences and/or the total of your life's experiences can impact your career decisions. A single experience could reinforce your current career path or totally change its direction. Career-defining experiences may include tragedies, everyday moments, or successes. A friend of mine lost a young sister which inspired her mother to start an organization to support grieving parents. Olga Kotelko joined a running club at seventy-seven because she was lonely, and ended up earning twenty-six world records in track & field. Tony Hsieh was forced to sell a company he had started after the business deteriorated. This apparent failure gave him time to think about what he wanted, and eventually, led him to create the company Zappos, the online shoe retailer he later sold to Amazon for $1.2 billion in stock.

The cumulative effect of your experiences could impact your career choices—where you grew up, the schools you attended, your family and your relationships with them, your experience with power structures, your attitudes toward finances and wealth building. Take time to ponder how your experiences have influenced you. We all have naturally built filters based on our experiences. Acknowledging these filters helps you be receptive to opportunities.

Since many of our waking hours are spent working, separating life from work (or creating a work/life balance) is a challenging undertaking. What may make more sense is to align your work with your identity, so that it provides you with a sense of purpose and is better integrated with your life.

If you are open-minded, your experiences could lead to meaningful career destinations. Consider the following three behaviors to help foster your open mind:

1 **DIMINISH PRECONCEPTIONS**—Don't let previous negative experiences prevent future possibilities.

2 **MEASURE FEARLESSNESS**—Average is the middle. It isn't the best. To rise above average, there must be risk. To risk, one must be fearless, but with a consciousness of outcomes.

3 **ADHERE TO AUTHENTICITY**—Know who you are, then stick to it, no matter the circumstances.

8

How do I find what I love and make money from it?

The most essential consideration in your career is to find something you LOVE to do. This doesn't mean that you will love every single aspect of what you do. There are tasks in every job that you may find unpleasant. Your goal is to find a job that you love overall. If you don't love what you do, you will experience any number of negative feelings, from anger and frustration to low self-esteem and unfulfillment. I truly believe that we are all uniquely suited to at least one career, but it is up to you to discover what it is.

You may fall into one of these three categories:

1   You know what you love and have defined a career. That's amazing! No need to read the rest of this FAQ!
2   You love certain activities, but don't see how they could become professions.
3   You have no idea what you'd love to do as your career.

If you're in the second group—you love certain activities, but they are not inherently income earning—no worries! The activities you love to do can clue you into what jobs you'd love to do. What if you're great at playing with new apps, love dancing at clubs, or feel happiest when you're at the beach all day?

Let's look at a technique you can use to extract potential jobs from activities you love. First, create a table with three columns and ten rows. In column one, create a list of things you love to do. No activity is off limits! To help you evaluate the things you love most, avoid thinking about financial compensation and focus on these questions: What would I do if I won the lottery? If all jobs paid the same wage, what would I do?

Next, consider the core attribute of each activity that makes you love it. Write that down in column two, next to the activity. Lastly, think creatively about how that root activity could be translated into a task in a job. Put that in column three. It may or may not be the exact same activity, but by re-contextualizing it, you may discover a new possibility.

Following is an example of this type of chart for some of my passions.

Things you love to do	Core Attribute	Job Responsibility
Travel to experience different cultures	Interest in cultures, enjoy traveling	Manage a global team
Take photo excursions in urban spaces and in nature	Observant, creative, adventurous	New product development in design or other visual fields
Meet new people at parties	Extrovert, good communicator, public speaker	Company Evangelist or Sales Person

Of course, you could be more literal and call row #1 a journalist, row #2 a photographer and row #3 a party promoter, but we are assuming the literal answer is not a job option for you. It's about translating what you might think of as a hobby into a job responsibility. Using this method, you could extract a list of tasks or responsibilities you enjoy that could bubble up into a job description.

If you fall into the third group, you could start with the exercise above, but will likely need further exploration.

9

Will my career be able to support my lifestyle?

The question is really, "What is more important to you, assuring you can afford a certain lifestyle or assuring you love your job, no matter what it pays?" It doesn't have to be an either/or answer; you can find a happy medium on that continuum. If you're concerned that your salary will not be enough to afford the lifestyle you envision, consider creating a budget. A budget will help you be realistic about your income and expenses.

Lifestyle expenses can include:

- **SPOUSE**—Are you married or do you expect to marry? Will you support your spouse and your family, or will you both contribute to family expenses?
- **CHILDREN**—Will you support children? Do they have any special needs?
- **OTHER RESPONSIBILITIES**—Are you responsible for others outside of your immediate family such as elderly parents? Do you have pets?
- **PERSONAL CARE**—Do you regularly spend money on hair salons or barbers, nails, a gym, dry cleaning, clothing, gifts, etc.?
- **HEALTH CARE**—Will you need to get health insurance or meet a deductible?
- **LOCATION**—Where do you plan to live—city, suburbs, country—and what is the cost of living in that location?
- **TRANSPORTATION**—Will you commute to your job? Work at home? Travel for your job? Own or lease a car?
- **PROPERTY**—Will you buy or rent? What expenses will be incurred to maintain your living space?

- **SOCIAL LIFE**—Do you like to attend sporting events, concerts, parties, dinners, etc.?
- **TRAVEL**—Do you plan to go on vacations on a regular basis?
- **HOBBIES**—Do you play an instrument or sport, have a garden or collection, brew beer, craft, buy the latest gadgets, or buy art?
- **SAVINGS**—How much will you contribute to a savings plan each month? Consider an auto-deduction directly from your bank account to make sure this happens.

There are many online tools and apps that can help you create and maintain a budget. Your bank may also offer budgeting tools.

10

How do I evaluate if a job is right for me?

A job is the kernel of your career. Ensuring that a job is right for you can be challenging! Following is a breakdown of the practical considerations to evaluate. The most important consideration is whether your values align with the company that hires you. Also, assess your "gut" feeling, or in other words, what your instincts are telling you about the job. They are just as important as what your mind tells you.

The five key factors of a job to evaluate are:

1 **ROLE**—What are the basic requirements of the job?
   - **JOB DETAILS**—What are the title, description, tasks, reporting structure, skills, education, and experience?
   - **HOURS**—Do the start and stop times and days of the week work for you? Are the total hours per week, including expected paid and unpaid overtime, reasonable?
   - **COMPENSATION**—What are the salary, benefits, and other perks, such as free food, gym memberships, training, and conference attendance, or the ability to work on innovative projects?
   - **RESPONSIBILITY**—Is it a leadership role for a large team or an individual worker? Are there late-night calls? Will you be making critical decisions? Will you be managing big budgets?
   - **TEMPERAMENT**—What temperament is required for this job? Working well under pressure? Negotiating with warring factions? Managing politically charged encounters? Patience and fortitude?
2 **LIFESTYLE IMPACT**—Will there be any positive or negative changes to your life and your family?

- **LOCATION**—Do you have to move? Do you prefer a location with shops, restaurants, etc. or an isolated corporate campus?
- **COMMUTE**—Is it long or short, during rush hour peak? What mode of transportation will you use?
- **BUDGET**—Does your expense allocation need to change?
- **HEALTH**—Will there be negative impacts to your health because of stress, long hours, night shift, bad eating, lack of exercise, etc.?

3   **COMPANY**—Will you feel good about working for the company?

- **VALUES**—Do your values align with the company? If you feel being green and supporting innovation are the most important values, does the company agree? What does it mean if they don't? This is extremely important to job satisfaction!
- **REPUTATION**—Do they have a good reputation in the industry and beyond? Does their name on your resume halo positive branding to you?
- **FINANCIAL STABILITY**—Is the company on stable financial ground? Are there major industry changes that could impact the bottom line?
- **SIZE**—Is the size of the company and the office a match for you? How many people will you be in contact with on a daily basis?
- **WORKPLACE**—Are the ambiance and design of the workplace suitable to you? If you are used to working in corporations, moving to a nonprofit might mean a drastic difference in interior design. Will you work from a cubicle, office, long table with others, sofa, or from home?

4   **PEOPLE**—What is the potential for building beneficial relationships with the employees and vendors?

- **SENIOR MANAGEMENT**—Check out the C-suite (executives with the word "chief" in the title, i.e. CEO, CMO, COO) and the Board of Directors. Do they have a good track record? Do you like their management style? Is there a good relationship between the C-suite and the Board? What is their public reputation?

- **SUPERVISOR**—Do you expect to get along with your direct supervisor? This is critical. Go with your gut instinct on this and, if possible, get feedback from others who have worked for your supervisor.
- **COLLEAGUES & VENDORS**—Who is in the office with you? Are these people you would like to spend time with, learn from, and support? Are the vendors reputable, and do they work well with employees? (I was in a situation in which a vendor was so cruel to a colleague that the colleague was in tears!)
- **ORGANIZATIONAL STRUCTURE**—Is it flat, hierarchical, or matrixed? Is it bureaucratic, or is communication smooth throughout the organization? Will most of your day be spent working alone, in teams, or in meetings?
- **NETWORKING**—Is there an opportunity to expand your network?

5　**GROWTH**—How will the job contribute to your overall career plan and set you up for your next position?

- **PROMOTABILITY**—What would be your next role if you were promoted? What is the possibility of that happening?
- **VISIBILITY**—Can you take on projects outside of your sweet spot to grow and explore? Will you be able to communicate your success throughout the organization?
- **SKILLS & KNOWLEDGE**—Will you be able to learn valuable on-the-job information and hone your skills?
- **CAREER EVOLUTION**—Can you see the possibility of a long career, even if that isn't your primary plan? Are there other jobs at the company that also excite you?

11
How do I know if I'll like a job if I've never done it?

This is certainly a reasonable question! How can you make a major life decision about what job you'd like if you've never done it? The best way to answer this is to approximate as best you can what doing that job would be like. Following are six tools you can use:

1   **JOB DESCRIPTIONS**—Read job descriptions from several companies listed on online job boards, LinkedIn, and on the career sections of company websites.

2   **JOB SHADOWING**—Follow someone who does that job for a day. You can arrange this through organizations like Big Brothers/Big Sisters, or by finding a contact in a company that has the position.

3   **INFORMATIONAL INTERVIEW**—Talk to people about their experience in that job.

4   **RESEARCH**—Look up the job in the Occupational Outlook Handbook, at BLS.gov, or at Glasssdoor.com to find out more about salary, available positions in your vicinity, and future growth of the role.

5   **INTERNSHIP**—The best test to determine if a job is right for you is to intern in that position. Find internships through the career services center at your school or through your contacts.

6   **FREELANCE**—Get hired as a freelancer on a per project basis to assess how you like working there.

You may try one or several of these techniques, think that you love the job, get hired, and still not like the job, but taking these steps will minimize your risk. Also, these experiences will help you determine whether you like the job or not more quickly.

If you have no idea what job you'd like to test drive, start by creating a list using techniques one and four, or by examining the things you love to do.

12
Is college the right choice for me?

If you're a high school or college student, or a professional considering a career change, you may be asking yourself this question, but education and training is an integral part of every career. Even if you have completed a college degree, you may consider a more advanced degree or a degree in another field at some point in your career.

College is a big investment and extensive research is required to find the right college and the right program. Whether or not college is essential for your career can be determined by answering the following four questions:

1   Will your career progress be facilitated by a degree, as opposed to working in an entry level job in the field?
2   Is a degree required for your occupation of choice, such as an architect or nurse?
3   Does the college have a good placement record for your field? This info should be provided by the college and can be cross-checked by researching third party's assessments of job placement rates.
4   Is there valuable non-degree information and experience to be gained in college that is not otherwise available? There does not have to be a one-to-one correspondence between what you learn in college and what information you need for a job, but be clear on your expectations.

To answer these questions, you may have to conduct intelligence gathering.

13

Will my college education prepare me for a job?

The purpose of college

Your college education can serve the role of training you for a specific job. Alternatively, it can provide general knowledge not directly related to a specific job. Sometimes, it will do both! It's acceptable to start college not knowing what job you'll get when you graduate, but be clear about what you expect from your college experience and degree. If you expect to get a job based on the training you'll receive, check the educational requirements of the job you have in mind. Confirm the universities placement metric—the percentage of graduates that get jobs in their field after graduating.

Today, because a college education is so expensive—tuition at a private four-year university costs $33,480 annually—most students want to ensure a job upon graduation.[8]

Value of a degree

A recent survey by Pew Research Center showed good news and bad news regarding the perceived value of a college education. The bad news: 65% of those with a Bachelor's Degree stated someone with less education could learn to do their job.[9] That means these graduates are not fully utilizing what they learned or can't find a job that matches their educational credentials.

Worst of all is that "just 16% of Americans think that a four-year degree prepares students very well for a well-paying job in today's economy," with 51% thinking it prepares students "somewhat well."[10] As noted, higher education has value beyond job preparation, but it seems like there must be a more efficient way to better prepare students for the professional world AND provide general knowledge and personal growth.

The good news: employment is rising faster in jobs that need more higher education. "Occupations requiring average to above-average education, training, and experience increased" by 68% from 1980 to 2015.[11]

"Most two-year and four-year college graduates think their experience was very useful:

- "Opening doors to job opportunities: 53%
- Helping them develop specific skills and knowledge that can be used in the workplace: 49%
- Helping them grow personally and intellectually: 62%"[12]

The perception is that college is valuable for personal growth, and degrees are required for preferred jobs, but the cost of a college education is being questioned. Will the university system evolve in the next five to ten years to provide a more comprehensive and economical solution? Will state or federal support help reduce costs? Time will tell.

Nancy Stuart offered the following pieces of advice about preparing for your career during school.

> Institutions of higher education have long recognized their responsibility to establish campus career centers staffed by trained professionals to help prepare graduates for careers. The services available range from help with resume writing and interviewing skills to job search strategies and individual advising.
>
> More recently, various databases have become available to help job seekers explore their options. CareerBridge, Career Beam, and Indeed are just a few of the internet-based tools that can be used to expand the reach of prospective employers and employees. Other social media sites, like LinkedIn, are available without a subscription and can be utilized to maximize a job seeker's network.

Students should not wait until their senior year to make use of college career centers or online resources. As soon as freshman year, interest assessments can be administered to help students determine career paths they should consider. Faculty advisors are also a rich resource for career counseling, and many universities have methods to link current students with alumni working in the field. Requesting an "informational interview" with a professional in your desired career is a great way to network and gain experience, as well as learning critical career information.[13]

14

How is the higher education system structured?

Although we most likely don't think of it as such, the higher education system in the United States, like other consumer product markets, is segmented by product type and consumer demographics. The education product is generally segmented into three tiers:

1 "200 or so highly selective schools with national, and even international, reputations"[14]
2 "[L]arge regional powerhouses...Usually public, with names that often begin with 'University of,' these schools have strong reputations in their home states..."[15]
3 "[N]onselective public, community, and private for-profit colleges that admit nearly every paying applicant...They vary greatly in quality...Some of these places, especially the private for-profit ones, seem to be little more than a scam, recruiting students, taking their government-funded loans and offering them a degree of minimal worth."[16]

The lack of general awareness about the structure of the higher education market, and the risks of investing in some ill-founded or fraudulent operation, leave many at risk of trading their life savings (or going into debt) for nothing.

In addition to the risk of purchasing an ineffective product, those whose families who haven't attended college will likely not get the chance. "The chances are greater than 70 percent that an American will not attend college if his or her parents do not have a college degree."[17] This further extends the gap between rich and poor.

Why is that a concern? Because the level of education of our country has a direct impact not only on individual life experiences, but on our growth and success as a nation. "The country's rapid growth during [the 20th] century—the rise of industry, the development of technology, the dawn of a vast middle class—would be hard to explain without acknowledging the spread of education as a cause.[18]

The improved education of U.S. citizens has not been sustained. After a peak in the 70s, during which the U.S. was ranked number one in attainment of college degrees, "it [now] ranks 14th, having fallen behind many other industrialized nations."[19] We can't expect a prosperous country without the faithful education of all, especially with the coming changes in the job market.

15

How could my student loan impact my career and lifestyle?

There is a crisis in student loans. In 2013, "Americans owed more than $1.3 trillion in student loans at the end of June, more than two and a half times what they owed a decade earlier."[20] To put this into context, this is more than the mortgage crisis of 2008. This averages out to a large debt for each graduate. "The median borrower with outstanding student loan debt for his or her own education owed $17,000 in 2016…A quarter of borrowers with outstanding debt reported owing $7,000 or less, while another quarter owed $43,000 or more."[21]

How might these statistics translate to impact your career and lifestyle? Studies have shown that graduating with a large debt has life changing consequences in three key areas:

- **CAREER CHOICES**— "Twenty-five percent of borrowers said they worked more than one job because of their student loan debt. Thirty-four percent took a less desirable job, 36 percent worked more hours than they wanted, and 37 percent worked outside their field of study."[22]
- **FAMILY LIFE**— "By 2012, about 31 percent of the millennials in the study were married and 33 percent had at least one child." As compared to the previous test group, "46 percent had married and 41 percent had at least one child…"[23]
- **LIVING SITUATION**—In the test group, "23 percent were living with their parents."[24]

In my humble opinion, we should not have to make the trade-offs of taking a less than ideal job, delaying the start of a family, and living with parents to get an education! With the potential of negative career and lifestyle impacts due to student loan debt, is investing in college worth it? It depends.

The good news is that it can be calculated. Mark Kantrowitz, student financial aid expert, has devised a simple formula for determining the value of a student loan. That is, will the debt you incur provide a good return on investment? Will the college degree translate into a job that pays more than one you would have taken without a degree—including the cost of the education?

The formula states that if half of the salary increase (net income after taxes) over the non-college job can repay the loan in 10 years, then the student loan was a good investment. Following is an example of how the formula can be applied:

> [T]he average starting salary for a bachelor's degree recipient in the humanities was about $45,000 in 2015... That compares with about $30,000 in average income for high-school graduates—or a $15,000 difference. After considering taxes, the net increase is about $9,000. Half of that ($4,500) is about 10% of gross income and would be enough to repay roughly $35,000 in student loans over a 10-year repayment term.[25]

For such a large investment, it is important to plan and make some calculations rather than just assuming it will be worth it.

16

What are informal sources of education?

Non-degree education

With the prevalence of free information on the Internet, much foundational knowledge can be learned outside of the framework of a university.

If you're just looking for information, not a college degree or college experience, the following is a short list of sites that offer free information typically included in a traditional liberal arts education:

- http://edX.org
- http://khanacademy.org
- http://alison.com
- http://udacity.com
- http://codeacademy.com
- https://ocw.mit.edu/index.htm
- https://itunes.stanford.edu (requires iTunes)
- http://ocw.jhsph.edu
- http://coursera.org

Perpetual learning

Because of the rapid changes in our society, we can no longer expect that a college education will provide the information required for our entire career. Expect that your career will require perpetual learning in the form of training and other sources of education. In a study conducted by Pew Research, "many see personal upgrading as a constant: More than half (54%) of adults in the labor force say it will be essential for them to get training and develop new skills throughout their work life in order to keep up with changes in the workplace."[26]

The career timeline has changed as well. When my father retired at 62, he retained his lifestyle. Workers today and in the future, will likely work until they are much older. "The concept of career is being shaken to its core. Employees now enjoy the prospect of 60-year careers. Yet at the same time, the half-life of skills is rapidly falling."[27] Employers are considering how to address this issue, but it is ultimately up to you to ensure you have the relevant skills at each point in your career.

Your career direction will likely shift frequently to align with the rapidly changing needs of the market. As the authors of *The 100-Year Life* point out, "42 percent of surveyed respondents now believe their organization's employees will have careers that span five years or less."[28] This suggests a strategy that requires your constant awareness of what influences the job market and your ability to adjust accordingly.

Career Stories & Archetypes

We reviewed definitions and other practical considerations. But the concept of career goes even deeper. Careers can be expressed as stories, biographies, myths and archetypes that are engrained into our culture. Whether someone has a famous career, such as Steve Jobs, or sits next to you at work, we can learn from their experiences. We'll share the career stories of a few recent graduates and those who are mid-career. I will also encourage you to write your own career story. Get your keyboard ready!

17

What are the career perspective archetypes?

While conducting interviews for this book, I listened to many career stories. I categorized these stories into archetypes that reflect the approaches people had taken to cultivate their career. Being aware of your career perspective archetype can help you assess how to direct your career. Your archetype is influenced by your nature and your current circumstances, and it can change over time. As you read the four types below, consider which one matches you.

Decisivist—Unflinching about their path

If you are a Decisivist, you were born to do what you do. You have a natural, irrepressible talent or vision for your career or a clearly identified external reason for pursuing it, such as taking over a family business or following the tradition of joining the armed forces. Whatever your reason, you have no doubt about what job to seek (or be given). The Decisivist may have an easier time if they are driven by talent or vision, and a harder time if they take an externally imposed role without question.

Think of Michael Jackson's extraordinary talent for dance, music, and entertainment. He was a star even within a family of talent! David Marriott is an example of someone who "inherited" their role. He took the reins of the international hotel chain after his father retired and grew it into the largest hotel chain in the world.

Rooter—Just looking for a paycheck

As a Rooter, your career is focused primarily on stability. Your goal is providing a steady income through a "day job." The role you have at work is less important to you because you find your satisfaction through non-professional interests such as family, social life, hobbies, or side gigs.

For example, a former team member had a very vibrant life outside of work. He was a volunteer fireman, always had a home improvement project in progress, and was a very involved dad to his young son. His job was a small part of a very full life, so what he did for an income was irrelevant to him.

In another case, I worked with a super talented and smart administrative assistant. He could easily have moved up in the company, but instead preferred his role. When I asked him why he didn't try for a more creative role, he said he needed a stable income and benefits because he ran a club promoter business. He wanted a predictable, relatively low-stress day job to support his primary interest. As it turned out, through several rounds of layoffs over the years, he remained at the company, while countless VPs, directors, and managers were let go!

Situationist—Internally-aware, searching for context

If you are a Situationist, you have a sense of self and your unique expertise, but you have not discovered how to apply this to a job. Translating your interests and skills into a way to make money is challenging. If this is you, you need to spend more time Intelligence Gathering—as opposed to introspection—to understand how your skills and abilities fit into the job market. Everyone may be a Situationist at some point in their career, especially during a transition to a new career.

Alex, who offers one of our mid-career stories, has a clear sense of self and is an accomplished professional, but at this stage in his career, he is defining what role in the current marketplace is best for him. He has the right approach—talking to people, researching the market, and exploring new dimensions of himself.

Experimenter—Requires self-assessment or learns through doing

If you are an Experimenter, you are characterized by changing jobs frequently, working side gigs, and/or exploring a wide range of roles. While the Experimenter enjoys the act of discovery, this perspective may be a permanently preferred learning method or be adopted temporarily because of a need for more introspection.

As an Experimenter, your preferred learning method is to do the job before deciding if it's the right fit. It may be challenging for you to decide if a job is for you by research alone, you may prefer to learn in a cross-disciplinary fashion and try several different jobs or gigs before choosing. You are constantly consciously or subconsciously collaging experiences that could, in the long run, coalesce into a unique role. You may not know the result, but you always follow your immediate interests. For you, success lies in the fusion of a unique combinations of interests.

Alternatively, your experimenting may be because you're not be clear on where your talents and/or interests lie. You may require introspection to uncover what's valuable to you and define your skills, knowledge, and interests. Self-assessment tests and techniques could help you through this discovery.

People who are serial entrepreneurs are good examples of Experimenters. Richard Branson, the billionaire behind the multinational Virgin Group, tried numerous, seemingly unrelated businesses that were unsuccessful before he became a great success. As a dyslexic, he was not successful in school, but learned through doing. Even today, he spans a wide variety of industries with his companies Virgin Records, Virgin Vodka, Virgin Health Bank, Virgin Money and Virgin Galactic. In true Experimenter spirit, he continues to try new commercial and philanthropic ventures.

Lee is a great storyteller who engages his listeners, partly because he's had literally hundreds of jobs in various fields—gas station owner, insurance broker, bartender, caterer, and male dancer to name a few. He didn't take the time to explore what was most meaningful to him, but through trial and error, he found his niche and today is a successful restaurateur.

18

What is the value of documenting my career story?

Telling stories is a decidedly human activity. We tell stories to memorialize our history, prioritize and give structure to an endless stream of moments, and share our experiences to connect emotionally. For similar reasons, it's valuable to document your own career story. A professional in transition will have a longer career story than a recent graduate, but even if your career story is short, it is still an important practice. If you are a recent grad, focus on your internships, freelance jobs, and volunteer experiences.

Documenting your career story will:

- Provide perspective on how important milestones unfolded in your life.
- Recall key successes and failures and the lessons you learned from them.
- Allow you to recognize patterns in your behavior and experiences which can help determine what works best for you.

Your career story is in progress, even if you haven't written it yet. It's formed by your experiences and influenced by where you grew up, your family dynamics, key life events, and your reactions to them. Your life experiences and interests contribute to your individuality and uniqueness.

How do I write my career story?

In sequential order, document your achievements, opportunities, challenges, insights, key influences, and feelings relevant to your work life. Think of your career story like the script of a movie. It has a beginning, middle, and end and is built from scenes. There is conflict and resolution. There may be a complex layering of themes, or it could be straightforward.

You are the star! Imagine who would play your part in the movie! While doing so, know that you can change the story line at any moment. Also, keep in mind the final scene of your career story. How do you want to be remembered? What contribution do you want to make to society?

Write a little each day or binge write it all at once; whatever works for your style. Then, make a practice of updating your career story on a regular basis.

What can you expect from this writing practice? Writing your career story is essentially a self-reflection tool. You may start to see patterns, or note the significant influence of people on your behavior. Once these factors are clear to you, you can decide if you want to continue, modify, or eliminate them. It's difficult to be an objective observer of yourself. Writing creates a third entity that is more easily observable.

Own your career story

To better understand the value of career stories, we'll hear how career coach Rachel works with career stories. She says:

> I see too many people trying to hide a crisis or a traumatic event in their lives in fear that if anyone within their professional network discovered it, somehow it would be a shameful revelation. I take the opposite approach. I coach clients to own their stories and use them as fuel to drive their passions or as street cred for their chosen fields, if they're connected to their stories.
>
> If you've made it through a rough time with wisdom and empathy, others will take notice and be inspired. They will be drawn to you and your honesty, rather than run screaming. Now of course, there's a dance in sharing. Emotional intelligence is necessary to best know the right time and place to share when you're building relationships. This takes time to develop, so don't worry if you stumble.[29]

As Rachel points out, we need to include our successes and challenges in our story to understand the value in each.

19
What are examples of recent graduate career stories?

Next, we will hear the budding career stories of several college graduates. Will's story is first and represents the challenge that many college graduates face at the start of a career: aligning the knowledge and experiences of college with an actual job. It's a critical step that receives precious little attention. As we discussed earlier in the book, college can primarily serve one of two goals:

1 Teach specific skills that are designed to facilitate employment, or
2 Provide knowledge and experiences that drive personal growth.

If a student is not aware of this distinction going into college, they may be confused when they graduate.

It doesn't appear that this is clearly communicated in the college education process, particularly, when the goal is personal growth. How does going to college for personal growth translate into an income-producing role upon graduation? Let's hear how Will takes on the challenge!

Will—Major change
Will's interest in stories inspired a passion for history. A Manhattan native, he attended a small college in Maine majoring in History and Government with minors in English, Education, and Italian Studies.

As luck would have it, his first internship—assisting a professor— occurred during the U.S. Presidential election. It was intriguing for Will to be on the inside track during an election year, taking calls with the New York Times and the Washington Post when they sought his professor's opinion.

After graduating, however, Will realized he didn't want to work in Washington. In fact, his interest wasn't in politics! Both of his parents are well-known painters in the art world, and Will had been exposed to art all his life. He watched his parents paint and attended gallery openings. He wasn't aware of his unique exposure to the art world until he moved to Maine and realized how much he missed being surrounded by art.

When he came home to NYC to visit, he couldn't wait to check out galleries and museums. Will knew he wanted to be a part of the art world, but in what role? He wasn't a painter, so he went on a journey to find out, prepared by the broad array of classes he had taken during his college education.

For Will, the value of college was in developing communication skills, such as how to be concise, both in his writing and speaking. This ability gave him confidence. When meeting with prospective employers, he found that these "soft skills" were key because that's what employers expected when hiring a recent college graduate. Will used college to go broad rather than to go deep, and it paid off.

To kick off his career in the art world, Will devised a plan. Through his network, he landed an internship at the Whitney museum. He continued reading about art and attending gallery openings. He spoke with alumni to gain their insights. He spoke with experienced people in the art world at openings and through his internship. Will was educating himself and learning about the industry while interviewing for a full-time job.

Quickly, Will realized the importance of networking, professional branding, and the ability to sell yourself to an employer. These were skills he could have practiced more in college. His friends, who were in more traditional fields, such as banking and finance, experienced a more linear path. They had internships in college that converted to full time jobs upon graduation.

After six months, Will landed a job. He is now looking to continue in the art field in communications or as a curator, but he may go to grad school.[30]

Josh—Practicalities of the industry

Like Will, Josh also had to reset his expectations when graduating. Here is his story in his own words:

I attended college with the original intent to become a film director. In school, I did a lot of production work and directing. The summer before I graduated, I got an internship at a local TV new station. My mom's friend suggested I contact the station about possible internships. The job was production-based— behind the scenes—a master controller operator.

First semester of my senior year, I participated in an exchange program for four months and studied in Los Angeles, CA, but I didn't fit in. I realized LA was not where I wanted to be after graduation, but it was closer to what I wanted to do production-wise. I know myself, didn't think I would like living there. I also imagined that I would eventually end up there because of my business, but I didn't want start my career there. It was a good opportunity because I explored the option with the security of being in school.

Four months after graduation, I was hired at the TV station where I was an intern, in the same role, as a freelancer. No benefits, but it was a stable position. I was living at home and on my parent's health care plan.

That was not my plan to return to the TV station. I tried looking for a job the summer before I graduated, but didn't find anything. I stayed at the TV station for 2.5 years. I continued looking for a job while at the TV station as I was looking for a more fulfilling role. I didn't have a clear idea of what I wanted to do, but I knew I wasn't in the right role. But I was only being offered the same role. Being a master controller operator was too behind the scenes for me. Also, the company was not providing a career path for me to my next role.

Then there was a company reorganization and my boss decided to leave. I felt loyal only to him as he took me on. This seemed like a natural breakpoint. I tried everything to get a job in New York City, but nothing materialized. I made plans with a friend to move back to LA.

For one of the jobs I applied to in New York, I got a call back from a major TV network for a supervisor position. The interview went well. Then I called every week to find out the status. A month later, I was told I was not right for the job, but another freelance position opened and they offered it to me. I accepted the job and didn't go to LA. It was literally the day before I was supposed to leave!

The job is similar to my old job, but I have a new title. My strategy is that I'll keep the job for the year and continue to look. It's for a well-known company and will look good on my resume. There are opportunities to move up and there are many people who have worked here for 10 years. I even helped a friend get a job here as well!

Is your dream still to be a director?
I don't know now. I can't picture doing it my entire life. I've realized I'm better at overseeing things. Maybe a Producer, as opposed to being on the set. The industry is very unstable: moving to different productions and struggling for your next gig. It's not the lifestyle for me.

Did you know how the industry worked when you were in school?
I knew in the back of my head, but it didn't become entirely clear until after school how directing worked. I knew that networking was important, but didn't realize it is completely who you know.

How do you search for a job?
I have a list of companies that are known to have a lot of jobs. After months of searching, I discerned the pattern of when they update their openings. I apply through LinkedIn or other job board sites.

What advice do you have for someone starting out?
Be open, be general. Think of doing completely different things to open your mind and meet a diversity of people. I went for an interview as a Tour Guide at Radio City! Being open has led me to opportunities.

Also, understand how important networking is. I was hesitant to network at first as I didn't want to think I owed something to anyone. But I realized how important it is to keep in touch and how meaningful relationships lead to something. It did show me the importance of keeping in touch.

And sometimes, just trust your instincts.[31]

Kevin's Friend—Overcoming the "no experience" challenge

Knowing your goals and where you are starting from is essential for taking the first steps towards launching your career or making a positive career change. Let's listen to Kevin's story about how his friend overcame the "no experience" challenge.

Every field requires specific knowledge and skills. However, some fields require skills that are more difficult to learn or innate talent to truly be successful. If your dream job is to be a professional singer, please make sure you can sing before you head down such a competitive and challenging path. If you can't sing on key or are tone deaf, education and practice will not help you. Fortunately, many careers aren't as challenging and innate talent-critical as being a singer.

When defining your career path, understand what you'll need to be successful and be realistic about your starting point. How do your knowledge, experience, and talents align with the expectations and requirements of the field? Your primary goal is to prove to those making the decisions that you are a great investment and they'd be lucky to have you. Once you understand your field's expectations and requirements, focus on developing your story for why someone should invest in you.

When my friend graduated from school with a Bachelor of Science degree in Business Management, she could have pursued many paths. Her real interest was in consumer products, specifically market research. Fortunately, she was living in New York City where there were many consumer product companies.

She had a lot going for her; great personal and professional interest, a college degree in a related field and she was living in a location with numerous job opportunities. Unfortunately, she had no direct experience to show she could do the job and she didn't know anyone in the field. Her starting point had many benefits, but there were still numerous challenges for her to accomplish her goal.

Since she couldn't land a job in her desired field, she searched for jobs with similar responsibilities that aligned well with her experience. She landed her first job as a marketing analyst and helped coordinate campaigns and events. The only relevant experience in this role was the word "marketing" in her title. A little over a year later, after a few months of research and numerous interviews, she took an opportunity as a database analyst. The role involved crunching numbers and analyzing advertising campaign data for a large agency. She hated it.

However, she realized this role had some responsibilities that were relevant to her goal of becoming a consumer products market researcher. She would pour through client data and prepared standardized reports. These reports were hiding important information she was seeing in the data. With her eye on becoming a market researcher, she proactively started adding insights she gleaned in the data to accompany the reports. The agency's clients loved the additional value, and my friend had her first true market researcher talking points.

Over the next two years she sought out ways to include research activities in her work. She also completed her Master's Degree in Marketing Research and connected with other professionals for advice. Eventually she was hired by a consumer research agency where her role was purely focused on conducting research with consumers.

Finally, after five years, her planning and focus paid off when she was hired by a top company in the industry to lead market research for their line of laundry detergents. She spent the next five years deepening her knowledge and expertise and eventually went on to work with major global consumer brands.

Regardless of where you are in your career, it's never too late to set goals and make a change. Your starting point may allow you to advance quickly towards those goals or you may need to spend time building new experience to prove your relevance. Also, be mindful of the market realities. If opportunities don't exist where you are, you may need to move to a location with more opportunities. Understanding yourself and your career goals will help you make informed decisions about what opportunities to pursue and what ones to turn down.

By building your story you'll understand your career and communicate your experience and talents to those you meet. Most opportunities happen from your outer circle, so craft your story and let others know where you're heading. Understand your goals and strengths, and research the path ahead before jumping in. You are the only person responsible for your career path, but many have walked your desired path, or something similar before you. Seek them out and learn from their mistakes to save yourself time. We get paid to do the things we don't enjoy, so focus on increasing your time spent on what you enjoy. Soon you won't think of it as work. That's the ultimate goal![32]

20

What are examples of mid-career stories?

The following are career stories of professionals in mid-career. If you're a recent grad, this will help you see how various career paths evolve. If you're at this midpoint in your career, these examples can help you gauge your experiences against those of others. Some themes that arise mid-career are: major career transitions to new fields, deeper dives in a specific role, and new journeys of self-fulfillment and public service.

John—The loyalist

John was displaced, as it's called, from his role as a top executive at a major corporation after twenty-two years. He expected to be an employee there until retirement and was ill-prepared to face the challenges of finding a new job. His first realization: he was not an expert in anything. His second realization: he didn't know himself.

During his tenure at the corporation, he was promoted to new roles at the company's discretion. John always accommodated. The company didn't consider if these were the best moves for his career. In all fairness, why should they? Their priority was the company's well-being. It was John's responsibility to guide his career. Examining who you are and discovering your purpose takes determination, humility, and patience. John was more loyal to the company than he was to himself, and when he was let go, that hurt him.

Ted—Becoming a master

Ted started his career as an analyst for a market research firm. He researched and wrote on the trends impacting certain industries. This information helped businesses decide which vendors to use and choose future products and investments.

Over twenty years later, he is still at the same firm, and he is still an analyst. Is that good or bad? Well, for Ted it's good because he loves his job. He was lucky enough to find it early in his career. As the company grew, so did Ted.

At times, as he saw he friends change companies, jobs, and even careers, Ted wondered if he was on the right path, but after some soul searching, he realized he was exactly where he was supposed to be. He likened himself to a baker. A baker makes bread every day, but every day he refines his craft and continues to perfect his bread. The same is true of Ted, except he is writing, researching, communicating, and thinking better. Mastering his craft down to the finest detail is the essence of his career.[33]

Alex—Finding zen

I climbed the corporate ladder, but my friend reminds me, "The mountains we climb are within, Alex." He reminds me that although I've climbed the mountains of Nepal and Tibet, the true struggles are in your own mind and soul.

I worked my way up from a junior designer to the head of the creative department of a major media company. As the company grew, I was promoted. Although I never attended college, I attained the job of my wildest dreams. Great big desk, called in my team of designers to brainstorm on my whiteboard the size of a wall, and won Emmys, awards from Wired, Apple and many other prestigious organizations. It was great conversation starter for cocktail parties!

I was brought into the company by a friend I worked with several years before. It seemed unattainable just five years earlier. I returned from an assignment in the military and realized my design skills weren't aligning with the market need. I took a part-time job at a major delivery service company, to get by. That was a blow to my ego.

I was driven by the critical voice of my father, "Get a secure job and work there until you retire." But that is what his generation lived by. Consistency and reliability were most important.

I am on a new journey now. What do you do after you've achieved your dream job? Ideals and morality...I am looking for a better connection between who I am and what I do—a sense of purpose. For me, the point of life is to fulfill your purpose and help others while you do it.

I don't have a roadmap, just trying many different things: creative conversations, digital products, photos, podcasts... Putting out feelers. Talking to people. Checking what's happening outside of a cubicle. You're able to think outside the box, when you're not in the box.

I've always itched to know what's going on here in the DIY culture of Brooklyn—this independent infectious energy. Today's generation is less interested in things, putting more value on experiences. They don't want to be prisoners to their possessions and instead take part in the shared economy.

But I don't feel armed up, don't have a utility belt filled with the tools I need. I'm figuring it out as I go. Deconstructing myself, peeling it all down like stripping floor wax. Sometimes I need a lot of elbow grease! Some days are scary. Then I get a phone call about a great opportunity or strike up a great conversation. I wonder if I'll know when to stop ruminating.

I don't know where I'm going to land, but I'm enjoying my current freedom. I have faith that it's going to work out. We see evidence that it does work out, if we are willing to do the work. I'm building networks, my community and I'm learning from it. It's a metamorphosis.[34]

Kathy—Nonprofit, profit, and back again

So, where would a college graduate with a degree in Chinese Studies end up? As a corporate marketing executive? Exactly.

After living in Taiwan for a year in High School, I took Chinese language courses in college, and then made it my major. After school, I worked at a nonprofit educational organization that focuses on Asia. While I enjoyed it, I was making $11k per year, and realized this was not sustainable. I decided to go to business school and work at a "real company" like my Dad did. I had some guilt about leaving non-profit, but promised myself that I'd make some money in the business world and then go back to non-profit when I was "old"—around 40.

So off I went to a top business school and got my MBA. I took a job at a huge financial services company, having no idea what I was doing when I started (fortunately they didn't know that!), and planned to stay only 2 years. I had no interest in living in New York City at the time, and figured I'd get a good company name on my resume and move on. Twenty-one years later, I finally left that company, and stayed in NYC.

I did go back to non-profit—when I was 50—and have fully enjoyed my new focus and direction. I work with a couple of different non-profits, and do some business leadership consulting to stay connected to business knowledge and trends. A lot of my work is volunteerism, which has broadened my view of the world, and put the important things into perspective.

Another aspect of my journey has been photography. When I was very young, my aunt told me that I had a "good eye" for photography. I wasn't sure what that meant but always remembered it. In 2007, I took a trip to Alaska with my first "real" camera and loved combining travel with photography. I found I was good at this photography thing—I guess my aunt was right!

At the same time, I was feeling a bit stale in my career. I didn't think I was creative, but I wanted to be. I decided to take on photography as a hobby, and it expanded my creativity in both my personal life and in my career. I've continued photography as a creative outlet into my "second phase" of life, and now it has become an integral part of how I travel and see the world.

I never actually expected that my promise to myself in my 20's would come true in my 50's, or that a comment from my aunt when I was a child would become a life passion, but when

WHAT IS A CAREER? | 51

they did, I felt very fortunate to have found fulfillment—even if it took half a lifetime to achieve![35]

Cathy—From art to heart

My father was a commercial artist, he died when I was nine. My mother worked as a secretary after he passed. She didn't have a college education nor a desire for a career.

Because of my family circumstances, from an early age, it was important for me to work and generate an income. In high school, I was babysitting and worked in a plastics spray nozzle factory in town. I took an aptitude test in high school that assessed I should work outside as a forest ranger. The idea of working outside was appealing to me, but I continued to college at the University of New Mexico and studied art. I had an interest in making things, and my parents had encouraged my artistic side. The University had a jewelry department and I discovered I enjoyed it a lot. I learned the basic techniques.

After graduating, I moved to Chicago and found a job in jewelry design. I worked in a couple of jewelry factories and learned two lessons. First was how to speed production through tips I learned from the experts from all around the world that worked there. I could size 80 rings in a day instead of just one. Secondly, from these guys, most of them immigrants, I learned about the immigrant experience. My social consciousness expanded.

I met my husband-to-be, Bill who was attending art school in Chicago. He was originally from New York, so we both decided to move there. After moving in, we had only $20 left in our pockets. The next day, we both went out looking for jobs and miraculously both found jobs!

After several minimal pay jobs in jewelry factories, at 35 we decided to have a child. Although my midwife was very good, I ended up in the hospital during our son's birth.

During my stay, I saw immigrant women being deprived of their rights in the hospital.

Interested in parenting, at the encouragement of a friend we joined a new mothers support group. Listening to their stories, thinking of the immigrant experiences I witnessed in the factory and in the hospital started changing my thinking. It was these life circumstances that made me want to change what I did for living. The immigrant population was amazing to me. There is nothing braver than to leave your country of origin. Bill is third generation American, so I knew of his family's story as well.

When our son was born, I stopped working, and Bill supported our family, but after three years, I thought of attending social work school as it felt closer to my heart than jewelry. Bill was 100% supportive about my career change, even though it would be hard to afford it.

I took a course at Hunter and decided to apply there. The first time I applied, I was rejected, but a professor suggested I apply again, but to the "group work" curriculum. It made sense, because I was involved in several groups which were in a way my introduction to social work: Al Anon, dieting groups, and parenting. I did well in social work school and understood it.

I never felt good enough as a jeweler. I never felt like a good artist. I had the examples of great artists like Bill and my father. I knew I would never be as good as them. I wanted to do something that I could be great at doing.

After graduating with a degree in social work, the more I learned, the more I liked it. I went from one job to the next and felt confident. I learned so much from different populations.

Several jobs and years later, Bill was encouraging me to start my own practice. I decided to keep my current job while starting my practice. I met a woman who had contacts at large institutions. She connected me with clients who needed support after the events of 9/11. I called insurance agencies and created contracts with them as my office was near the 9/11 site. I would race between my day job and my new private practice. After one year, I quit my day job and worked on my practice full time.

I like what I do and can't imagine retiring. I changed my life at 40. What you decide at 19 is not what you have to do the rest of your life. You're never too old change your career.[36]

Teena—Entrepreneur from the start

I graduated January of 2011 as a communications major and followed an unconventional career path. While in college, I went to a bible study and heard about Production Assistant (PA) jobs for a locations scout from a member of the group. That got me into the movie/TV/commercial business in Washington, DC. Production Assistant work gave me professional media experience as an undergrad.

I packed my car, drove to LA from DC with a friend to gain more experience working in the industry. Once in LA, I found a cheap room far in the valley. To find PA work, I checked Craigslist, Facebook, LinkedIn, and went to various meet ups and parties to meet people and get my foot in the door.

In 2017, you don't need to go to school if you want to work in the entertainment industry. One way to learn the trade is by networking and volunteering on independent projects. A lot of these types of projects happen while on hiatus from regular TV show production schedules or between bigger movie/commercial projects. If there's an opportunity for good paying gigs, the producer you worked for during that down time could then hire you, giving you paid PA experience.

I worked as an assistant for a movie producer and as a PA for TV commercials and films. I realized I preferred working for producers in the office. This brought me closer to being in the corporate world and appealed to me because of the better hours.

I decided after three years of working in production that I didn't want to continue this type of work. The entertainment experience I gained had provided me the tools needed to create my own show, if I wanted.

I worked as a temp at Google and realized working in corporate isn't all boring. There is a lot of stigma about working an "office job," but I found there is no universal atmosphere. You can have a good life with money and decent work hours.

After working four years in an office setting, I started exploring what kind of business I could start. I came to my dream job journey piece by piece. It made sense for me to work in tech, but I love music. I wrote songs and played guitar after work, then played open mics, then shows, then started recording. Every piece of my creative occupation journey began piece by piece.

In talking with people, I came to new ideas which informed the trajectory of my songwriting business. Right now, I am in the process of business development, defining market needs, costs, and assessing our service offerings. We expect to launch PopWrite Inc. mid-2019.

I progress by putting one foot in front of the other, growing organically, with passion fueling me every step of the way. As my own business evolves, I still must prioritize my current day job.

What advice would you give to a student in college?
Get experience while at school and learn through trial and error. My interpersonal communication course taught me how to network to gain opportunities. One extremely valuable piece of information my professor gave me was to take

notes about each person you meet while networking—write three words. In the TV business, you must meet on average 100 people to get one job. You must be friendly to make connections. Another piece of the plan to gain work is to have people vouch for you. Go to parties, lunches, and mixers. Practice talking about yourself—marketing and presenting your best attributes. Through trial and error, you'll learn through your mistakes.

Do any job that you can in the industry you desire, and learn it. Always take on new responsibilities. Keep upping your game until you make it to the big leagues. Spend 18 months to two years in your first job, then leverage your experience into something you're passionate about. While working on your dream job, you most likely will need to keep a day job.

But be sure you are at least happy in that day job. Pay attention to yourself—how you are feeling and know what keeps you going. A couple of years ago, I was depressed because I didn't know what my passion was. Find what gives you meaning, what makes you feel alive. Don't be afraid of sadness or stillness because the negative emotions inform you. Only you can take care of you.

Ask people what they see in you. Insights from others is always valuable. Find unique ways of engaging with people and pay attention to that information. Seek info from people about other industries to broaden your horizons.

You can be anything you want to be. Choose to live outside of a cubicle.[37]

Employment Structures

Now we will broadly explore the definitions of each of the employment types: employee, contingent worker, small business owner/entrepreneur. This will help you consider which employment type is most relevant for your goals and personality type. Throughout your career, you'll likely experience multiple types, if not all.

You can choose to work in various types of employment—as an employee, a contingent worker, or a small business owner/entrepreneur. The primary challenge, if you don't have a full-time job, is to maintain a reliable income. That means developing a client base or having a pipeline of projects.

There is much we are not covering here, particularly about small business ownership/entrepreneurship and vocational careers, but there is enough info for you to evaluate which employment type is right for you in your current situation.

21
What are the three main categories of employment?

This book focuses primarily on the life cycle of full-time employees, but before detailing the steps of the full-time employee life cycle, let's review the three main categories of employment: employees (which includes full-time and part-time work), contingent workers (which includes temps, contractors, freelancers, and gig workers), and small business owners/entrepreneurs.

The main distinction between the groups is whether the worker is looking for employers or clients. Although there is some overlap, employees, temps, and contract workers generally are looking for employers, while freelancers, gig workers, and business owners/entrepreneurs generally are looking for clients or projects.

Some situations involve overlapping categories of employment as well. A designer may have a full-time job but subsidizes their income with freelance design projects for a roster of clients. Someone else may be contracted as a business writer but has a passion for writing humor and finds gigs on the side. There isn't one correct way to fulfill your employment needs.

Employee
An employee is someone hired by an employer and can be full-time or part-time. A full-time employee works a minimum of thirty hours per week, with an unspecified end date. A part-time employee is typically defined as less than thirty hours per week. Employees can be hired directly by an employer or through a recruiter. As an employee, you sign a contract with a company, and in return, receive a salary (usually paid bi-weekly), benefits (which include health care, paid leave, sick days, 401K, other financial benefits such as stock options, and other "perks" which could include free lunch, free access to events, or other incentives).

As an employee, termination from the company is at the company's discretion, but they must abide by federal and state laws. Employees are expected to follow directions and not own any work contributions made. For instance, if you invented Facebook while you were working on a special project as an employee for Apple, you would have no rights to that idea; Apple would own the intellectual property.

As an employee, you may work on site or remotely. If you work from home by request of the company, not for your own convenience, the company should pay for all, or some portion of, your space and equipment. In this case, it's best to engage advice from an accountant to claim your benefits.

We'll come back to the situation of employees later, but in this section, we'll focus on the other two, more complex, employment types.

Contingent workers

The contingent worker category includes temps, contractors, freelancers, and gig workers. The U.S. Bureau of Labor Statistics defines contingent workers as "people who do not expect their jobs to last or who reported that their jobs are temporary [without] … an implicit or explicit contract for ongoing employment."[38] Let's review each type in further detail.

Contractor

As a contractor, you will sign a contract and typically work a specified number of hours per week. Unlike full-time employees, contractors receive few, if any, benefits (most likely just health insurance), and their employment is based on a contract for a limited amount of time—typically not more than eighteen months, although it might be extended beyond that. A contract is typically arranged with a third-party vendor that manages payroll and benefits, so you are not directly hired by the company. Contractors typically receive a greater salary that a full-time employee would in the same role to compensate for the lack of benefits, the unpredictability of the employment and in some cases, extensive subject matter expertise.

Freelancer

A freelancer is a cross between a contractor and a business owner. Unlike a contractor, freelancers are usually hired for projects rather than a specific time-period. As a freelancer, you are typically hired for a project with a deadline that signals the end of your engagement. Occasionally, you may be hired for a specified length of time—for example, to fill in for someone who suddenly left or to help a team with an excessive workload—but this is not the norm.

As a freelancer, you are not an employee, and as such, you are responsible for all aspects related to your employment: health insurance, marketing, account and project management, invoicing, retirement account, etc.

A freelancer is also like a business owner in that they manage the client relationship. Although they may be predominantly hired on a per project basis, many freelancers form long-standing relationships with clients which can help guarantee consistent work. A successful freelancer will usually have relationships with several companies to keep a steady flow of business, which is the greatest challenge for this style of work.

In general, a freelancer has less security than a contractor. Work may be conducted on-site at the client's facility or off-site at the freelancer's office or home. Freelancers are sometimes referred to as "solopreneurs."

Gig Worker

Some experts indicate a shift in the workforce towards what is termed a "gig economy." The gig economy is characterized by online marketplaces through which individuals find suitable project work. For example, there is a website called Upwork where you can find a gig for research, writing, design, marketing, or other related business services. After signing up and creating a profile, you can browse posted project requests and send proposals. The website then takes a commission out of the contract in exchange for having facilitated the engagement. Other similar websites may have different business models or other fee arrangements.

A gig worker is like a freelancer in that they work on a per project basis. Unlike a freelancer, the intermediary may take over some of the responsibilities such as business development, marketing, invoicing, and insurance.

Business owner/entrepreneur

The last employment option is running your own business. The business owner/entrepreneur has the most responsibility of all employment types. The success of the business ultimately rests on your shoulders, and your decisions impact your staff, vendors, and customers. As a business owner/entrepreneur, you decide everything about your business: the products or services offered, the customer base, the brand, the strategy, the development processes, and the financial policies.

The primary difference between a contingent worker and a business owner is that with your own business, you can expand by hiring more employees to take on larger projects. The distinction between the two is also a question of branding. If you market yourself as a contingent worker, clients will think of you as an individual and most likely not offer you large projects that would require a team.

That is not to say that a freelancer does not hire anyone. They might hire an attorney for contracts, an accountant for taxes, a financial advisor for retirement savings and other investments, and an assistant to manage administrative duties. However, these hires tend to be 'as-needed' rather than full-time employees.

22
What is a contractor?

The contractor role is closest to a full-time employee role in that an employment contract is signed. The agreement differs, however, because it is for a specified amount of time, typically not longer than eighteen months. The number of hours per week can vary, as can whether the contractor works on-site or off-site. In most large corporations, contractors are hired through a third party that manages the hiring, invoicing, and benefits.

Contractors are utilized for the following reasons:

- Cover for a temporarily absent employee
- Specialized expertise
- Short-term project needs
- Budget constraints

Contractor jobs are not always advertised. You can find out about them through your network or from vendors that hire contractors. Today, there are also several online marketplaces for contractors such as Toptal, Flexy and Carrot. Contractors can technically work in any role, but the most opportunities tend to be for consultants, technology experts, and project managers.

The contractor life cycle

The life cycle of the contractor can start with a full-time job or another way of building a relationship with a company. An employee who loses their full-time job may be rehired by the same company in a contractor role. This allows the company to save money on benefits and have more flexibility in terminating the engagement. On the balance sheet, it is typically more beneficial to label workers as contractors, as opposed to employees, as they can then be categorized as an advertising or marketing expense (depending on the role). This is more favorably perceived by financial markets which is hugely important if it is a public company.

If a contractor (or a freelancer, for that matter) meets several criteria set by the government, they can be deemed an employee. Following is a summary of the criteria from the Fair Labor Standards Act (FLSA):

1 **INTEGRAL TO THE BUSINESS**. If the work performed means the worker is economically dependent on the employer, not in business for himself or herself.

2 **MANAGERIAL SKILLS**. Does the worker's managerial skills affect that worker's opportunity for both profit and loss.

3 **INVESTMENTS IN FACILITIES AND EQUIPMENT**. If a worker's business investment compares favorably to the employer's that they appear to be sharing risk of loss, this factor indicates that the worker may be an independent contractor.

4 **OPERATING AS INDEPENDENT BUSINESS**. To indicate possible independent contractor status, the worker's skills should demonstrate that he or she exercises independent business judgment.

5 **PERMANENCY STATUS**. Permanency or indefiniteness in the worker's relationship with the employer suggests that the worker is an employee, as opposed to an independent contractor.

6 **THE NATURE AND DEGREE OF CONTROL**. Who sets pay amounts, work hours, how the work is performed, whether the worker is free to work for others and hire helpers.[39]

23

What is the gig worker/ freelancer life cycle?

The "gig economy"

The gig economy is characterized as "networks [or marketplaces] of people who make a living working without any formal employment agreement—as well as by the increased use of machines as talent."[40]

The process for sourcing project-based work has changed with the onset of online marketplaces. To reflect that change, the term "gig economy" evolved to describe the phenomenon, and with it, the "gig worker." (The term gig economy entered recent terminology during the 2008 financial crash when workers were taking any "gig" they could to make ends meet.)

How prevalent is the gig worker? There is conflicting information, partly because it is difficult to document contingent workers in general, and gig workers more specifically. The current data available from the Bureau of Labor is from 2005, but it is expected to be updated by early 2018.

Though initially pundits predicted the end of the full-time job and the rise of the gig economy, some believe that that is not playing out just yet. A recent J.P. Morgan Chase Institute study found only about 4.3% of U.S. adults had ever earned income from an online "gig platform" as of June 2016, and growth in gig platforms has fallen steadily in the last three years.[41] Regardless, the gig worker does exist and has delivered an economic impact.

On the other hand, a report by Deloitte claims that 33% of today's workers are freelancers. By 2020, that number is expected to be 40%.[42] If that prediction is true, that means at some time in your career, you'll likely be a freelancer. That is, if your skills are not completely replaced by a robot or an AI solution! The strategy, at least at this stage, is to evolve your skills and your career to be flexible and take on any of the employment forms.

Why is this shift from employee to independent worker happening? Well, it is the natural progression of the workforce. Advances in technology and the drive for profits continue to shape the marketplace structure, and as per Deloitte, building a workforce on a freelancer base is beneficial for two reasons:

1   The cost structure of paying with purchase orders is preferred over salaries.
2   The availability of talent; data scientists, for example, may not be willing to move to a company's remote headquarters but could be engaged remotely and temporarily.[43]

What's the difference?

"Gig worker" and "freelancer" are sometimes used interchangeably. Other interpretations claim that a gig worker is simply today's freelancer. In some cases, the gig worker is positioned as a subset of a freelancer—a term sometimes used to cover all non-contingent roles.

When a distinction is made between the two terms, the gig worker and freelancer differ in how the work is sourced. The key difference is that a gig worker works on projects that are posted on an online service marketplace. Their "client" is the online marketplace, and payment typically is distributed through that marketplace. A freelancer can do gig work as well, but they generally find work through direct connections with clients or through an employment service, and they are paid by that client/service. The gig worker and the freelancer engage in project-based work, but the freelancer may also be commissioned for time-based work.

Gig worker life cycle

Gig workers are a relatively new phenomenon born from the technological disruptions in various service marketplaces. Entrepreneurs have found certain marketplaces ripe for technological solutions that facilitate communication between those seeking services and providers. Most famously, Uber solves the urban customer's need for on-demand transportation, and AirBnB introduces room/house owners to temporary renters. TaskRabbit and Handy offer home maintenance workers like house cleaning, painting, or window washing. FlexJobs connects people for a wide range of part-time business services, such as research, copy writing, or customer service.

The life cycle of the Gig Worker starts with defining your skill set, then researching the best marketplace for those skills. Joining a marketplace is typically free, as they are trying to attract a large mass of workers. Marketplaces require submitting profile info (and possibly a portfolio), as well as a method to accept payments. Accurately complete the profile with all info, as your profile is your marketing document. It's the first encounter a potential client will have with you.

If the marketplace is branded as an exclusive site, offering the top tier of gig workers in a field—such as Toptal which hires the top 3% of consultants—there may be a vetting process. This could include skill testing, verification of employment, or other methods of ensuring your professional acumen.

Once signed up, it's a matter of branding yourself on the platform. Most platforms offer a rating system that lets the project owners comment and rate your work upon completion. That's beneficial to you once you've completed several projects and have a high rating, but the challenge is how to get started. The following tips might help you gain traction more quickly:

1   **RESPOND IMMEDIATELY**—Sign up for notifications, if available, and respond to project posts with concise proposals.

2   **ACTIVELY SEARCH**—Use advanced search, if available, to narrow you search to the projects most relevant to your skill set, and conduct that search regularly.

3   **PERSONALIZE**—If available, provide a cover letter or note explaining how you're the right person for the job and how you'll execute the work.

4   **RECOMMENDATIONS**—If the platform allows for recommendations, ask clients to submit one at the close of every project.

If not, assemble recommendations that highlight your top three skills and submit them with the proposal, if allowed.

5 **BE ACCESSIBLE**—Offer several ways to get in touch (text, phone, email). Include your contact info on every correspondence, and respond immediately to messages.

The gig employment structure is essentially freelancing, but through an online marketplace, which serves as the intermediary between you and the client. This system has its pros and cons. The positives are:

- Access to opportunities which would otherwise require a significant marketing budget to discover.
- Freedom to work from home, which eliminates or reduces commuting time and expenses, and/or allows more flexibility for family responsibilities.
- The chance to test the waters in an occupation, with very little commitment, before deciding to commit.
- Flexibility to work in multiple roles.
- The possibility of supplementing income while working on a passion project or your field of interest.
- Increased opportunities for those not in metropolitan centers.

The negatives are:

- Global competition drives down rates.
- Inconsistent work makes it challenging to predict income.
- The difficulty of establishing a reputation when starting out (more established participants get preference based on reputation).
- The lack of guidance on how to manage benefits, taxes, and other issues related to running a gig business.

The freelancer life cycle

As a freelancer, you share similarities to a small business owner. The job search phase of your life cycle will be about finding clients, not jobs. In addition to joining the relevant online marketplaces (as a "gig worker"), you'll establish relationships with clients who will ideally provide you with repetitive work. To that end, while freelancers still need self-awareness, relationships, and a clear definition of the types of clients they are looking for, they will also require additional skills in marketing, PR (public relations), customer service, legal, accounting, and training.

Following are the steps in a typical freelancer life cycle:

1 **SELF-AWARENESS**—Know what you do best and enjoy most. Define your unique expertise and hard and soft skills.

2 **RELATIONSHIPS**—Follow the best practices for building your network. Always be prepared to meet a prospective client on vacation, at family gathering, or on a job.

3 **DEFINE YOUR CLIENTS**—Research the industries and companies you'd like to have as clients and create a list of prospects. Consider the current and future state of the world/industries, locations, pay scales, and use of freelancers in the industry.

4 **LEGAL**—You'll need legal advice when starting your company for forming your business entity (Corporation, Limited Liability Company, or other variations), creating basic contracts, and assessing complex contracts presented to you by large companies.

5 **ACCOUNTING**—Set up an accounting system. You may consult with an accountant or do it yourself through online services such as FreshBooks or QuickBooks. Automate your hour tracking and billing as much as possible to ensure accurate invoicing and prompt payments.

6 **MARKETING & PR**—As a freelancer, you'll likely not have a big budget for marketing. Most your work will come from word of mouth. When you do a great job, request that your

client refer other clients to you. Your primary marketing will consist of emailing or calling prospects and building your brand on the appropriate social media channels such as LinkedIn, Facebook Business Pages, Twitter, and other outlets—basically wherever your prospective clients spend the most time. Announce your successes, such as the launch of a new project or landing a new client. Share your expertise on a blog, in conferences, or other forums.

7 **CUSTOMER SERVICE**—To ensure repeat business, provide excellent customer service. This means treating your customers with respect, bringing positivity to the engagement, being reliable, and communicating concisely. It's costly to gain new customers, so treat your current customers like gold!

8 **TRAINING**—To stay competitive, note when you need to upgrade your skills with training or other education. This can align with trends in the marketplace. Occasionally, review job posts for your role to note skill requirements. You may not be looking for a job, but it's better to stay current with the baseline skills required for your role.

24
How do I build a client base?

If you are not looking for a full-time job, you are always on the lookout for new clients. The process of finding clients differs from finding a job and requires an ongoing process. The best way to build a client base is to define your goals, then reach your prospects through a measurable plan. To build your client base, follow the cycle of defining and researching your target market, reaching your market, building relationships, and promoting your successes. Further on in the book, you'll learn about defining your brand and positioning, which is the groundwork for your marketing, PR, and advertising efforts.

The end goal, and the most efficient way to find clients, is for them to find you. There is nothing better than having a client contact you asking for your services! This doesn't happen overnight, but it can happen over time, as you build your reputation through successful PR.

(Please note that the following is just meant to give you a sense of what it takes to build a client base. Many books and articles have been written on this topic which is the crux of a business's success.)

Define and research your target market

Although it may seem obvious, the first step in building a client base is defining your target market. That's what "marketing" means: defining the subset of people—or market—that are going to purchase your services. To determine your target market, define the attributes of your target client: industry, location, size, values, reputation, etc.

Let's say you're an illustrator with an interest in illustrating food packaging. Start with a list of the top ten food manufacturers that fit your requirements. Get to know those ten companies through intelligence gathering—checking their websites, checking industry publications, Glassdoor.com, talking to people in the industry that you found through your network, taking photos in the supermarket of their products, and researching the illustrators they use. Your goal is to become an expert in this industry and find out all the key factors about your prospective clients through your research.

Reach your prospective client

Once you know who your client base is, devise a marketing strategy for how to reach them. Continuing with our food illustrator example, one strategy might be to attend a meetup or seminar for entrepreneurs in food manufacturing. Look for opportunities where your clients will be present "in bulk" to meet more potential clients at once, and learn more about the industry. In addition to the networking example above, you may consider the following.

1 **EMAIL MARKETING**—Send personalized emails to prospects, including unique insights about the company and person you discovered while researching. Present a clear "call to action"—the behavior you want to elicit from the recipient whether that be a phone call, an in-person meeting, more information, a connection to someone in the company who'd purchase your services, etc.

2 **SOCIAL MEDIA**—Select key platforms (Twitter, LinkedIn, Instagram, etc.), and post content to boost your recognition and reputation. Post valuable content at predictable intervals, as well as successful case studies.

3 **SOCIAL MEDIA ADVERTISING**—Use targeted marketing on Facebook or other channels to sell your services or webinars.

4 **SEARCH ENGINE OPTIMIZATION**—Create ads based on keyword phrases that are placed in search engines.

5 **PR**—Submit story ideas through a press release to relevant publications for journalists to write articles about you, or to get quoted in articles as a subject matter expert. Look for interviews or speaking opportunities by starting with your

alumni groups, organizations of which you're a member, local businesses, school, or government agencies.

6   TRAINING—Offer free training sessions on relevant topics to your target market. Using the illustrator example, you might offer a webinar about the color trends for next year, and market the offering on Facebook. The training session will help build your list of prospects.

7   MARKETPLACES—Post your profile and/or portfolio on online marketplaces that your target market frequents. Don't dilute your presence by posting everywhere. Select key sites, keep your content fresh, and track your success rate. Using the illustrator example, you could post your illustrations on the image-centric social media platform Instagram with relevant key word tags.

Build relationships with clients

Every project and every interaction throughout the life of a project provides an opportunity for building a relationship with your client. Every time you engage with your client, you can increase their trust in you through reliable behavior, on-time and on-budget deliverables, resolution of any conflicts or confusion, and stress-free, positive experiences.

While you should always be in the moment with your client, you eye is also set on the possibility of future engagements and referred business.

Communicate successes and be thankful

Upon completion of a project, thank your client for their business and provide them with a forum for feedback. The feedback could be in the form of an email—possibly automated through an email marketing service—or you could provide them with a short survey through an online survey service.

Communicate your successes on your website, blog, or favorite social media channels. If you see a bigger story based on the project you completed, you can present it as a story idea to a publication. For example, if you just completed an illustration for a tin of chocolate covered ants, and your illustrator friend is working on an illustration for hot and spicy grasshoppers, you have a story about an insect food trend! The story might focus on how insect snack food manufacturers are resorting to illustrations, instead of photography, to minimize the "insect-ness" of the food. Submit the story to writers who have written about food trends or illustration techniques.

25
What Is a small business owner/entrepreneur?

Unlike the other two employment options—employee or contingent worker—being a small business owner (SBO)/entrepreneur involves a great deal of responsibility and commitment. You can't switch back and forth between running your business and a full-time job like you can between contracting and full-time work. In that respect, it doesn't follow a "life cycle," but is more of its own work/life experience. Starting a business requires research and planning. It also takes a certain type of person—full of energy, passion, and vision—to ignite a new venture.

As an SBO or entrepreneur, you are looking for clients or customers as opposed to employers. In this respect, it's like a freelancer who looks for clients, but since a freelancer is one person, they don't require as much revenue as the typical SBO/entrepreneur.

What's the difference between an SBO and an entrepreneur? Although they are sometimes used interchangeably, there is a key distinction. An entrepreneur is looking to change the status quo within their market, to break new ground. A small business owner is looking to make an income by owning a business. Being innovative is not their goal; rather, they simply seek to provide a product or service. If you're interested in being a small business owner, it is possible to buy an existing business as opposed to starting it on your own.

Before you start your own business, consider the following key challenges:

1   **FILLING A NEED**—You must create a product or deliver a service, then market it to a customer base large enough to provide revenue to sustain your business.

- **WEARING MANY HATS**—You will perform every role of the business at the start (unless you launch with a team or partners).
- **DEDICATION**—You'll need to prioritize the business over all other obligations, until it's stabilized.

Small business survival rates

According to the U.S. Bureau of Labor Statistics, the following are survival rates for small businesses with employees. These numbers remain stable across economic crisis and industries.

Year	% Of Businesses That Survive
1	80
2	66
5	50
10	30

The key cause for a business failure is lack of capital, although there are other issues, ranging from lack of demand for the product or service to the wrong business model.

Key roles of a business

If you are starting a business by yourself, at first you will fill all the key roles in your company, from the "C-Suite"—CEO, CFO, CMO—to the assistant to the receptionist. Not everyone is suited to play all roles at once or to switch jobs abruptly from one minute to the next. You might go directly from negotiating a deal with the CEO of another company to taking out the trash! Following is an overview of most roles you'll need to undertake to launch your business:

1   **CEO (CHIEF EXECUTIVE OFFICER)**—As the highest-ranking officer, the CEO defines the business model, strategy, and vision and is the company's public face.

2 **CMO (CHIEF MARKETING OFFICER)**—Defines the marketing strategy and leads branding, marketing, advertising, PR, and social media initiatives.

3 **CFO (CHIEF FINANCIAL OFFICER)**—Defines the structure and manages the company's funds and expenses, provides reporting on the financial status, and from the reporting, determines what adjustments need to be made to assure future financial success. The CFO defines what funding is required and how to source it.

4 **COO (CHIEF OPERATIONS OFFICER)**—Handles the processes related to producing your product or service (less relevant when you are just starting).

5 **CTO (CHIEF TECHNOLOGY OFFICER)**—Creates and manages the technology platforms for your business, including the email client, your website, and any other technology needed to run your business, such as phone systems, asset storage, e-commerce, and an intranet, to name a few.

6 **HUMAN RESOURCES (HR) DIRECTOR**—Manages the employees and non-employee resources from hire to termination.

7 **CUSTOMER SERVICE REPRESENTATIVE/SALES ASSOCIATE**—Responds to inquiries about purchasing the product or service and handles any complaints/praise received from customers. For a service based company, a sales associate will fill a similar role.

8 **ADMINISTRATIVE ASSISTANT**—Supports administrative requirements such as scheduling, internal communications and correspondence, travel arrangements, some vendor management, and related clerical tasks.

9 **RESEARCHER**—Sources information to support the development of the business related to competition or industry status, and manages the data required to produce the product or service and related information.

10 **ACCOUNTANT**—Manages the bookkeeping, taxes, and day-to-day financial reporting.

11 **LAWYER**—Engaged when needed to review or create agreements with clients, vendors, services, employees, and realtors, or to handle lawsuits, patents, copyrights, and trademarks.

12 **DELIVERY OF THE PRODUCT/SERVICE**—This is industry dependent and most likely includes many people. For example, if your company's product is an app, you may start the business by working with a vendor who supplies the design and development of the app. As your company grows, you could bring those roles in house.

In terms of when and who to hire: first hire for the areas in which you have no expertise. For example, you'd hire a lawyer to review a contract, if you have no expertise in law, or an accountant, if you don't know how to file taxes. Define your own hourly rate. If you are spending a lot of time on tasks that you can hire at a lower rate than yours, and you have the funds, hire that assistant, researcher, or other person that your business needs.

Running your own business is a complex venture; the above hardly scratches the surface of what you need to know. The first step is to assess whether owning a business is suitable for you. If so, there is a world of knowledge out there to help you. A great first step is sba.gov which provides assessments and the basics.

How Do I Cultivate My Career?

26
Why is career cultivation important?

Before we discuss the aspects of your career that you'll cultivate—traditionally referred to as "career management," let's address why it's important. If you don't make a conscious effort to cultivate your career, you're leaving your life in the hands of others. Cultivating your career puts you in control of your destiny and you'll be:

1   Alerted to great opportunities that surface in your network.
2   Prepared, if you lose your job.
3   Aware of what your next promotion should be at each stage of your career.
4   Informed of when you need to reassess your skills and abilities to match the needs of your company and the job market.
5   Conscious of your career capital (that is the combination of your values, skills, and abilities).

Much of career cultivation is about forming good habits. If you form them early in your career, it will make it easier to drive your success. Good behaviors include:

1   Being conscious of your thoughts and feelings about your current job
2   Attending networking events and conferences
3   Staying in touch with your network
4   Being aware of company, industry, and global trends
5   Refreshing your skills and knowledge as needed
6   Managing your professional brand
7   Keeping your LinkedIn profile and resume current

Get into good habits early on. According to Charles Duhigg, author of *The Power of Habit*:

> Most of the choices we make each day may feel like the products of well-considered decision making, but they're not. They're habits...This is particularly true in our 20s, when so many of our habits are still up for grabs...How much money you make, how much time you spend with your friends and family, how well your body functions years from now—all of these, in many ways, are products of the habits you are building today.[44]

Self-Awareness

Who are you? Do you understand the components that define your identity, influence your decisions, and determine your path? Being self-aware is essential to your success. Your process of self-examination—exploring, assessing, and refining your identity—will last throughout your lifetime.

In career counseling, this effort is referred to as "assessment." A career counselor will employ a formal system of assessment to facilitate the development of your self-awareness and determine which jobs suit you best.

In this section, we will examine what contributes to your identity. You'll explore five dimensions of self-awareness: appearance, preferences, behaviors, achievements, and skills. Your goal is to synthesize everything you learn about yourself into a cohesive sense of self. From that knowledge, you'll formulate a coherent package to promote yourself to employers: your professional brand. Let's dive in!

Appearance

Your appearance includes your physical presence, how you maintain your health, the impact you make in person, and your physical expressions, including how you dress and walk.

27

How do I express my physical presence?

Today, 86% of jobs require that you sit at a desk with very little physical activity.[45] It's up to you to ensure you get the right amount of activity. It's recommended that the average adult get at least 150 minutes of moderate aerobic activity or 75 minutes of vigorous aerobic activity a week. Strength training exercises for all major muscle groups are advised at least two times a week.[46]

You could be stellar in several of the areas of self-awareness—possess emotional intelligence, be in good health, and have a great personality—but if you don't present well physically, the rest of your greatness may be overlooked. Your physical presence is the main contributor to the first impression you make, so make it count!

It's hard to be conscious of your physical attributes. The best way to observe these characteristics is to watch yourself on video. I suggest you videotape yourself presenting a speech and pay attention to the components below:

1   **CLOTHING**—Dress in your own style, but wear outfits that are appropriate for the occasion (e.g. business casual, business formal). If you don't know how to style yourself, consider hiring a fashion consultant. If that's not in your budget or feels like overkill, scan through blogs, podcasts, and magazines for fashion ideas. You may also consult the salesperson in your favorite stores. Let them know the occasion you're shopping for (daily work, interview, business presentation), and ask for suggestions. If you have the budget, utilize a tailor to ensure properly fitting clothes for interviews and other significant events. An adjustment to hem, arm length, or waist, can change the impression your clothes make.

2 **POSTURE**—Stand, sit, and walk with vertical alignment and positive energy. Do not slouch, puff out your chest too much, hunch your shoulders inward, or keep your hands in your pockets.

3 **FACIAL EXPRESSIONS**—Your facial expressions are their own language and should align with what you're saying to ensure you're not communicating mixed messages. Some people may have unconscious facial patterns, such as always constant frowning or a nervous tick. Observe your expressions on video, or ask a close friend if they notice any involuntary expressions.

4 **VOICE**—Your voice is expressed through several dimensions: volume (how loud or soft you speak), tone (the mood you set and the relationship it implies with your audience), rhythm (how fast or slow you speak and your pauses), and annunciation (how clearly you speak).

5 **GESTURES**—A gesture is a movement that imparts meaning. Properly using gestures to express yourself is part of your physical presence. Do your gestures work against you, such as nervously tapping your fingers or jiggling your foot, or do you intentionally utilize your hands to emphasize a point or nod your head to signal understanding?

Observing your physicality on video is a tool for aligning the image you have of yourself with how you look to others. Be patient with yourself. It takes time to make refinements to behaviors that you've developed over many years. Being conscious of them is the first step. Also, consider taking an acting class. Many of the considerations outlined above are part of the acting practice.

Preferences

Your preferences are the things that you've made a conscious decision to "like" above others. Are there activities or interests you enjoy, such as playing music, attending sporting events, or being in nature? Do you prefer people who behave a certain way or have certain characteristics? What values are most important to you? Family? Financial gain? Political justice?

28
What are my "situational preferences"?

I use the phrase "situational preferences" to refer to the inextricable dimensions of a job. Since they are inherently non-negotiable, know where you stand on each preference. If a job does not meet your minimal requirements for situational preferences, then it should not be considered. Situational preferences include, but are not limited to, the following:

1   **LOCATION**—The town or city where the job is located. Is it in a location where you will like being every day?

2   **HOURS**—Do the required hours fit your lifestyle? Is there too much unpaid overtime required? Is there flexibility for exceptions such as doctor visits or attending to family members?

3   **COMMUTE**—Do you have accessibility to transportation to get to the location? How much time and money are you willing to spend on commuting? Will your commute require stops, such as dropping kids off at school or picking up dinner on the way home? Are you OK with traveling during rush hour?

4   **DRESS**—Are you comfortable with the dress code?

5   **WORK ENVIRONMENT**—Do you like the office environment? Do you have enough light and space for your preferences? If you work from home, can you focus, or do you have to create a more distraction-free space? Do you have all the equipment you need to work from home (computer, fast internet, desk, etc.)? If not, how much of an investment will it require?

6   **COLLEAGUES**—Although your immediate supervisor and team will likely change, how do you connect with them? Also, consider your feelings about the rest of the employees that you'll work with frequently. In larger corporations, the culture and employees can greatly differ between departments.

7   **COST EXPENDITURES**—Does this job require any new purchases before you start? Will you need to purchase a car or pay other commuter expenses, such as a monthly train pass? Will you need to enhance your wardrobe to meet the dress code? Any other expenses?

29
How do I discover my interests?

What are your interests, the activities that capture your attention and keep you engaged? Knowing your interests will help you define what you'd like to do as a job. Following is advice from Angela Duckworth, author of *Grit*, on revealing your interests:

> How to discover your interests? What do I like to think about? Where does my mind wander? What do I really care about? What matters most to me? How do I enjoy spending my time? In contrast, what do I find absolutely unbearable.
>
> If you find it hard to answer these questions, try recalling your teen years: the stage of life at which vocational interests commonly sprout. As soon as you have even a general direction in mind, you must trigger your nascent interests. Do this by going out into the world and doing something. To young graduates wringing their hands about what to do, I say experiment, try. You'll certainly learn more than if you don't.[47]

It is a good practice to maintain interests outside of your job. Those interests can influence your next job, help you relax or de-stress, network, and explore new skills. In many cases, today's jobs, particularly in large corporations, can be very narrowly focused. Opening your mind to new experiences and activities outside of work will help you grow.

Following are some activities to consider:

ACTION

- Playing sports
- Playing an instrument or singing
- Creating art or crafts
- Starting a collection
- Cooking
- Sewing
- Acting class
- Dancing lessons
- Gardening
- DIY home improvement

INTELLECTUAL

- Taking a course
- Studying an art movement and visiting museums
- Writing a novel or keeping a journal
- Participating in local politics

SOCIAL

- Watching sports
- Concert going
- Joining a MeetUp group
- Volunteering for a nonprofit
- Attending theater

As you develop your interests, consider if you'd like to earn money from them. This can be referred to as a "side hustle," or something you do to make money outside of your primary job. For example, as an interest, I love cooking, but I don't want to become a chef or earn money from this interest. For me, it's relaxing and creative. On the other hand, I love drawing, and have earned money from that interest.

30
What if I have many interests?

If you have many interests, good for you! There is no reason to limit yourself, especially at the start of your career. Build on each interest using the process that is best for you. You may decide to formalize your approach to each interest. For example, to improve my art skills, I decided to spend at least an hour a day drawing. A classroom setting may work for you, or a less formal meetup discussion with friends who share your interest.

Your combination of interests is what makes you unique and is essential to understand when crafting your professional brand. Maybe you like music and animation, so you produce music videos. Maybe you're a writer that is passionate about social causes, so you write the website copy for an advocacy group. Be open and imaginative in considering how your interests can be combined to create a new vision, product, or process.

As you hone in on your interests, shift to focus your time on what will produce results for your career goals. To become an expert in a specific topic requires many hours. If your goal is to attain expert status, at some point, you'll have to narrow your interest—which could be in a combination of fields.

For example, I worked with a colleague who is extremely talented. He has multiple degrees and interest, ranging from technology to opera, has worked for major corporations, and was excellent in all of his roles. However, unfulfilled by corporate life, he decided to go back to graduate school for photography. He discovered his true passion. Now, his attention is focused on his particular interest in biographical portraits.

Rachel is a career coach. Let's hear her advice on managing your interests:

In trying to figure out your expertise or unique area of interest, let me remove the pressure for you. First—you don't need to choose one thing. And second—expect it to change over time. I wish somebody told me that when I was in college. Perhaps I wouldn't have changed my major five times looking for my perfect passion—at which I was already an expert! Instead, focus on things you've always loved to do.

What are the things you do—that when you're doing them, you lose track of time and space? Do more of those things every day and the ideas will come to you. And when they do come, trust your intuition. Go toward what you want to do and not what you think you should do. Nobody ever built a meaningful life by following a path they thought they should take. You've worked too hard to give up the prospect of a meaningful life so get to it![48]

31
What does "finding your purpose" mean?

Purpose is the sense of meaningfulness and connectedness experienced in response to a specific job or your career, or in the words of Merriam-Webster dictionary, "the action for which a person or thing is specially fitted or used, or for which a thing exists."[49]

Deciding if your career provides you with purpose usually requires conscious consideration. Purpose is born of play and exploration. As explained by Angela Duckworth in her book, *Grit*, it means we have gone beyond our own interest and are in some way serving the needs of a greater audience. When you hear people speak about how they love their profession or that it doesn't seem like work, they have found their purpose.

Professional coach Annie has this to say about finding your purpose:

> In my view, this means that you have found something which you feel passionate about, which makes you feel motivated about and energized by. It's a place where you feel mainly at ease; it sits comfortably with your values and you can play to your strengths there.
>
> When you find your purpose, you know it. It's no longer work or a job—it's life and you'll give your all to it.[50]

Becoming clear on your purpose will improve your life experience. In his TED talk, Scott Dinsmore stated that the 20% of people who are happy and passionate are doing work that embodies who they are.[51] This happy group has three things in common:

1 They have become an expert on themselves, understanding their unique strengths, values, and experiences
2 They do the impossible
3 They surround themselves with other passionate people.

What can you do that is unique? How can you reach for the sky? Where can you find a work environment full of colleagues that will elevate you?

Don't feel pressure about finding your purpose. Be gentle on yourself. Your purpose may not be singular and all encompassing, either. At different points in your life, you may feel different purposes. It's possible to feel more than one purpose at a time. You may not have the skills or experience to reach your purpose right away, or it may be already within your grasp. As Annie told us above, we will know it when we find it!

32
How do you define your core values?

Your core values are your guide—your own personal philosophy. Core values inform your behavior, particularly in challenging situations when ethical or time-pressured decisions must be made.

Some examples of core values are:

- Relationships
- Financial Gain
- Compassion
- Creativity
- Justice

Imagine you are offered a job with a high salary, but it requires travel and consequently very little time with your family. If "family" is a core value and "financial gain" is not (or is lower on your list), you would decide not to take the job. However, it doesn't mean you wouldn't take a different job with high financial gain.

If you need more examples of values, look to religion, politics, philosophy, literature, art, and film. Can you discern values in their themes, stories, and doctrines? Using these templates as a guide, document your own values. They can be individual words or sentences and should be easily memorable. Make a practice of reviewing them from time to time to assess if they are serving your needs.

New experiences and influences throughout your life provide you with opportunities to identify, question, and re-prioritize your values. You see the world around you through the lens of these values. This foundation helps form your definition of right and wrong, determine whom you can trust, and understand what's most important to you. Essentially, your values help guide your decision-making, so understanding them in the context of your professional life is important.

Let's listen to Kevin's story of how his values helped guide him during a challenging career evolution:

> When I was 25 years old, I set a goal to become a CEO before I turned 40. I moved to New York City and spent my early professional life constantly seeking new challenging opportunities that improved my business knowledge and skills. I actively sought out experts and mentors to extract their wisdom, and along the way, I learned how dramatically values differ from one professional or organization to the next.
>
> Celebrating wins, learning from failures, and surrounding myself with a diverse group of people and ideas broadened my understanding of business and the world. This journey fundamentally changed my core values, but you don't often realize these kinds of changes until you are tested.
>
> Twelve years after starting my professional career, I accepted an offer to become CEO of a small software startup. Over the next three years, I met some incredibly talented people and others whose proposals pushed ethical and legal boundaries. In this role, I was the person responsible for making the decisions. Often, despite analyzing every potential path and outcome, my decisions were driven by people I trusted, what I believed was "right," and what was most important to me and the investors, employees, and customers I served. The answer was driven by my core values that I had been honing and re-prioritizing over the previous twelve years.
>
> If you want to define your core values, start by questioning what's most important to you. The journey often teaches us more than the destination.[52]

Behaviors

How you behave is determined by many factors. Here we will look more closely at how to assess your personality type, emotional intelligence, and motivations.

33
What are personality types?

Your personality type is the sum of the preferences that define you. Knowing your personality type provides you with insights about which job categories you're best suited for, how you interact with coworkers, and how you make decisions.

The Myers-Briggs assessment is the most popular tool utilized in professional settings to assess personality types. As per the Myers & Briggs Association, the assessment makes "the theory of psychological types described by C. G. Jung understandable and useful in people's lives."[53] The assumption is that if we understand the lens through which we view the world, we will better understand our strengths and weaknesses. Each type is associated with a core behavior that is then paired with jobs.

The assessment is a multiple-choice questionnaire which results in a four-letter type. There are four dichotomous pairs which combine to form the sixteen types described by the Myers & Briggs Association. The pairs are:

1 **EXTRAVERSION-INTROVERSION**—Do you prefer focusing on the outer world or on your own inner world?

2 **SENSING-INTUITION**—Do you prefer focusing purely on the basic information you take in or interpreting and adding meaning to it?

3 **THINKING-FEELING**—When making decisions, do you prefer to first look at logic and consistency or at people and special circumstances?

4 **JUDGING-PERCEPTION**—In dealing with the outside world, do you prefer to get things decided or do you prefer to stay open to new information and options?

The Myers-Briggs assessment is a very complex tool, and I've only provided a quick overview here. It is worthwhile to take the full assessment to help you gain insights into how you get energy in a work setting versus what types of settings will drain you. It also helps you understand how you take in information, make decisions, and basically function throughout your day. These insights help you understand how you fit into group dynamics and team settings, both of which are common in today's workplace.

The Myers-Briggs assessments may be available through your career services office. Otherwise, search online for free, unofficial versions or paid, full versions of the assessment.

Despite the prevalence of the Myers-Briggs assessment as a guide to match you with a job, there have been questions as to the value of using it the workplace.

> Most of us are about average on at least one of the four dimensions, which means that we probably teeter on the edge between two (or more) types. Answer one of the questions differently, and you might fall into a different personality type. This happens about 50% of the time, according to some reports, which should further emphasize the importance of not using the MBTI to make any important decisions.[54]

Some new companies have candidates play games to provide insights into which careers would suit them best. For example, the company Pymetrics provides a series of simple games that test your levels of trust, risk aversion, planning capacity, and other personality dimensions. Based on your results, they suggest broad career categories that suit you such as Private Equity, Human Resources, or Operations. These results then link to job postings.

It can be informative to take these tests, but don't base your career decisions only on a personality or trait-based test. There are far too many parameters in any job or career to let a personality test decide, but they may provide insights to you about unrecognized personal traits.

34

How do I assure my psychological health?

Assuming you are starting from a point of good psychological health, how do you maintain it, especially during stressful times? According to Anita Morse, psychotherapist, it is a really simple formula:

- "Get enough sleep"
- "Spend time with nature"
- "Study how your mind works"[55]

Prioritize sleep

When working in the Los Angeles school district with troubled grade school children, Morse asked students to draw a picture of where they slept. The pictures drawn showed the students in their living rooms with the television on. They were living in tight quarters, sometimes in multi-generational situations, and were expected to sleep on the couch while adults watched TV. Their lack of sleep was directly connected to their poor performance in school and their difficult relationships with other students.[56]

I hate to overstate the obvious, but sometimes we take the obvious for granted. Today, many successful people declare themselves as needing only a minimal amount of sleep. An article in the Financial Post lists eighteen successful executives who claim that they sleep only three to six hours a night[57]. According to Harvard Medical, however, "not sleeping enough can cause poor health and lower perception and judgment."[58] Ariana Huffington became a proponent of a healthy sleep life with her book, *The Sleep Revolution*. She's right! The Mayo Clinic suggests that "adults should sleep 7-9 hours per night" for optimal performance.[59] There are some exceptions, but not many. "Researchers find that a tiny proportion of people, 1% to 3%, can get along fine on four hours or less." [60]

Commune with nature

Studies have proven what we know instinctually: being in nature has healthy psychological effects on us such as eliciting positive feelings and calming our nerves. Why does experiencing nature through a hike in the woods or stroll on the beach bring about therapeutic results?

The answer lies in the relationship between nature and mindfulness. Mindfulness is the practice of bringing attentiveness to the present moment: what you are sensing, thinking, and feeling. When we are in nature, there is an abundance of sensory experiences that put us squarely in the present. We are "mindful" of the scent of the ocean, the sun sparkling on the water and the roar of the crashing surf. Mindfulness is like hitting the reset button.

A clear example was demonstrated in a controlled experiment in which a team from Stanford "investigated whether [a] nature experience would influence rumination (repetitive thought focused on negative aspects of the self), a known risk factor for mental illness...[The] results suggest that accessible natural areas may be vital for mental health in our rapidly urbanizing world."[61]

The study also points out that by 2050, 70% of the world's population will live in urbanized areas.[62] Access to nature seems critical to ensuring the control of mental illness in urbanized environments.

So what can we do? Incorporate time for connecting with nature as part of your daily routine, even if that means staring at the clouds drifting by—if you live in a dense urban area. When feeling particularly stressed, or when trying to make difficult decisions, taking a walk on the beach or a hike in the woods might be the best remedy. A city dweller myself, I look at the sky and the river at regular intervals to stay connected to nature. A college professor of mine suggested that New Yorkers, like me, would all go crazy if it weren't for Central Park!

How your mind works

It's hard to keep something working properly if you don't know how it works. There are many aspects of how your mind and brain work—how we perceive the physical world, how we process emotions, how memory works, and how the brain evolved, to name a few. I'll highlight an explanation of how the brain maintains itself and one theory on the construction of the mind, but this is a very deep topic; these examples are just meant to pique your curiosity to study further.

Let's consider one aspect of the physiological mechanics of the brain. I'm going to paraphrase an excellent Ted Talk by Jeff Iliff, "One More Reason to Get a Good Night's Sleep," where Jeff describes how our brain maintains itself.

Iliff says all our organs require two essential functions:

1 Nourishment
2 Waste removal

The brain is not an exception, however, unlike all other organs, the brain waste removal function is not carried out by the lymphatic system. Instead, there is a system by which the blood vessels' exterior surface serves as transportation for cerebrospinal fluid (CDF), and that fluid transports the waste of brain cells.

Stay with me here! The most amazing feature is that this waste removal system for the brain, unlike all other organs, happens only while we sleep. Our brains are so busy all day, they can't take a break to clean the waste materials from our brain cells. They are only cleaned at night. As Jeff suggests by his title, all the more reason to get a good night's sleep![63]

Now, on to how our mind works. Another Ted Talk features Antonio Damasio on the topic, "The Quest to Understand Consciousness." Damasio defines consciousness as being constructed of two components: the mind and the self. The mind, he describes simply as "...a flow of mental images."[64] By "images" he means any sensory expression: visual, auditory, tactile, etc. The process by which these mental images are created—in highly simplified terms—is a neural mapping of the sensory input which is then further interpreted or enhanced by the brain.

Describing the self is a bit more complex. It is our daily physiological maintenance routines that serve as the anchor of self. Describing all the details of the self is difficult, as Damasio explains his theory:

> [T]o have a conscious mind, you have a self within the conscious mind. So a conscious mind is a mind with a self in it... If you're going to have a reference that we know as self—the Me, the I in our own processing—we need to have something that is stable...The things that have to do with what is known as our internal milieu—for example, the whole management of the chemistries within our body—are, in fact, extremely maintained day after day...And it is out of this...tight coupling between the brain stem and the body...you generate this mapping of the body that provides the grounding for the self and that comes in the form of feelings..."[65]

To reiterate, knowing how the mind works is one of the three principles of maintaining our psychological health simply because if we don't know how it's supposed to work, we don't know if there is something wrong.

As we transition to a world filled with less direct human interaction, how do we retain our connection with life, with what's real? One way is by bringing a consciousness to our actions and perceptions. There is not a hierarchy between the body and the mind, humans and animals; all is interconnected. How we perceive and interact with the world is a function of our integrated body and mind.

35

What does Emotional Intelligence mean?

Emotional Intelligence (EI) or emotional quotient (EQ) is defined as:

> The capability of individuals to recognize their own, and other people's emotions, to discriminate between different feelings and label them appropriately, to use emotional information to guide thinking and behavior, and to manage and/or adjust emotions to adapt environments or achieve one's goal(s).[66]

Why is this important for your career? First, being able to perceive your own feelings subsequently allows you to make the right decisions. Second, EQ is important for navigating the relationships and politics that accompany every job.

Learn to read your own feelings through self-reflection. In a busy office environment, you could be tasked with managing many relationships within a short time frame: instructing a direct report, communicating with senior leadership, managing a vendor, etc. Sometimes, one exchange can bleed into the next, or you may just get overwhelmed. Know when to take a moment to analyze your behavior or responses and take corrective action if needed. When you mess up, chalk it up as a lesson for next time.

Recently, I was on a conference call with more than ten people regarding a project that was delivered late; tensions were high, and fingers started pointing. Instead of joining the blame game, the leader of the call asked everyone to take a second and jot down what was the most important next step to get the job done. She noticed her own temperature rising, along with the rest of the team, but had the emotional intelligence to recognize it and reset the situation.

Although the primary responsibility of your job is to perform tasks and excel in predetermined skills, very rarely does that happen in a vacuum.

Navigating the world of office politics requires reading how people feel and delivering an appropriate response. In the workplace, the value of EQ is most often noted when providing feedback on performance, delivering difficult instructions, communicating an unwelcome message (such as layoffs), and in meetings and presentations with complex or emotionally charged subjects.

In these instances, be perceptive and note changes in non-verbal cues, as well as verbal statements that may be delivering conflicting information. For example, imagine that you are explaining a complex topic in a presentation. You note a perplexed look on some attendees' faces. You might pause to ask if everything is clear and get a "yes nod" response, but because you are receiving mixed messages, try another route to confirm your suspicions. Look for another way to describe what you're explaining. People aren't always aware of (or don't want to acknowledge) what they are feeling.

36
How do I respond to expectations?

At the crucial life milestones of graduating high school, finishing college, looking for your first job, or making a career change, there may be others who expect you to behave in a certain way. A recent theory by Gretchen Rubin has shed some light on how we respond to expectations. She formed this framework while researching habits and human nature for her book, *Better Than Before*.

Rubin's "Four Tendencies" framework provides insight into how people respond to expectations. Armed with this knowledge, you can make better decisions about how to address challenging expectations, like a parent pressuring you to pursue a particular career, or a spouse or partner placing demands on you during a transitional time.

Rubin divides expectations into outer expectations— "a deadline, a 'request' from a sweetheart"—and inner expectations—write a novel in your free time, keep a New Year's resolution.[67] She then defines four types of people as follows:

1 **UPHOLDERS**—respond readily to outer and inner expectations
2 **QUESTIONERS**—question all expectations; they'll meet an expectation *if* they think it makes sense—essentially, they make all expectations into inner expectations
3 **OBLIGERS**—meet outer expectations, but struggle to meet expectations they impose on themselves
4 **REBELS**—resist all expectations, outer and inner alike[68]

There is no right or wrong type. As with knowing your personality type, defining how you manage expectations is another tool that helps you understand your own tendencies. If you are an Obliger, it might be challenging for you to be an entrepreneur since setting your own expectations is essential to entrepreneurship. If you are a Rebel, it could be challenging for you to work in a formal corporate setting like a bank or law firm.

37

How can I understand my motivations?

There are several motivational theories which are the result of psychological research that will help you quantify what drives you. What makes you want to work? Is it to perceived as a leader? To be socially accepted? Or maybe you want to make a difference for others who are less fortunate?

Understanding what motivates you is important when considering the work environment, reporting structure, and responsibilities which will best suit you. Following are two motivational theories, one new and one traditional.

Maslow's Hierarchy of Needs

The Hierarchy of Needs is the traditional theory of motivation, developed by psychologist Abraham Maslow. It states that there are needs in human beings that progress linearly from basic survival to self-actualization. Until the first needs are met, the later ones cannot be considered.

1 **PHYSIOLOGICAL**—food, water, air, excretion, temperature regulation, sleep, clothing.
2 **SAFETY**—Personal: physical, psychological, emotional, and moral well-being. External: financial, property, and resource security.
3 **LOVE & BELONGING**—Relationships, intimacy, and connectedness.
4 **ESTEEM**—Confidence, achievement, and respect.
5 **SELF-ACTUALIZATION**—Morality, creativity, spontaneity, problem-solving, equitability, and realism.[69]

As you move through your career, you'll inevitably experience good and bad times. Your needs will shift relative to your situation in your personal life and within your work environment. Being conscious of where you on this hierarchy will help you focus your energy in the right direction.

Promotion vs. prevention focused

A new, more simplified perspective on motivation, with a career orientation as opposed to survival in life, comes from Heidi Grant Halvorson in her book, *Focus*. Rather than a pyramid of needs, she suggests that knowing your own focusing style, whether promotion-focused or prevention-focused, helps determine which companies and roles best suit you. Making the right match leads to improved job performance and the attainment of more value from your job.

Promotion-focused jobs are those that "offer advancement and growth. Consider fast-paced industries where products and services are rapidly changing, and where the ability to identify opportunities will be essential, like the tech sector or social media."[70]

Prevention-focused jobs "offer a sense of stability and security. You are good at keeping things running...Consider careers where your thoroughness and attention to detail are valued—for instance, as a contract lawyer or data guru."[71]

38
What is time management?

Part of your journey of self-awareness should include understanding how you manage time. This includes what hours of the day you feel most productive: Are you a morning or night person? Is your natural inclination to be late, early, or on time? Do you like to plan or act spontaneously? Do you track your time? Once you have a sense of what feels most comfortable to you concerning issues of time, consider how to better manage time in your professional life.

There are countless books and approaches on this subject. I won't make any suggestions other than to explore your inclinations. To manage your time efficiently, you may have to adjust your behavior.

I would encourage you to get into the habit of tracking your time, regardless of if it's required by your employer. Tracking your time will provide you with three benefits. First, you'll know how long it takes you to perform various tasks. When your manager asks you how long it will take to do something, you will know. Second, you'll be able to track your improvement. If you don't know how long a task takes, you won't know if you've improved your efficiency. And lastly, it provides the basis for a self-reward system and drives your success. If each day is just an eight-hour blur, it's hard to feel a sense of accomplishment. If you complete four two-hour projects in a day, you'll experience a sense of fulfillment.

39

What techniques can I use to unplug?

We live in a world of information overload. People living in cities can see up to 5,000 ad messages a day.[72] On average, we watch more than four hours of live television per day.[73] The time U.S. users are spending in mobile apps is continuing to grow…we're up to 5 hours per day on our mobile devices.[74]

In addition to being overwhelmed by advertisements and media,

> Americans work an average of 34.4 hours a week, longer than their counterparts in the world's largest economies. Adults employed full-time report working an average of 47 hours per week, which equates to nearly six days a week, according to Gallup. Nearly four in 10 workers report logging 50+ hours on the job.[75]

If we always live on the outside, we will never know who we are on the inside. To help, try making it a habit to spend a portion of each day unplugged from the world. How that happens is up to you. Some options are:

1 **MEDITATION**—This is the practice of calming your mind. Yoga, Tai Chi, and other disciplines specify how meditation is conducted. Meditation could also be facilitated through podcasts or apps.

2 **SILENCE**—If you're not comfortable with the practice of Yoga or meditation, spend some time each day in silence without any activity or inputs. Notice where your mind takes you.

3 **JOURNALING**—Write or draw the events that impact you each day. Don't worry if you don't consider yourself a writer or an artist. This is a tool for you to use for reflection.

4 **DREAM MANAGEMENT**—Document your dreams with a notebook by your bed. There are also apps and other technological gadgets that facilitate documenting your dreams and analyzing them.

5 **NATURE WALK**—Although walking doesn't detach you from the outside world, it does remove you from the usual inputs.

Achievements

Achievements describe situations in which you recognized a problem and proactively solved it. Achievements can be attained through life experiences (climb Mount Everest), education (earn a PhD), or professional work (become the CEO of a company).

40

What are my key professional achievements?

As you proceed through your career, continually document your key professional achievements as they occur. If you are starting out, use your internships, volunteer experiences, and part time jobs. Following are some questions to ask yourself:

- Did you receive some form of recognition (award, title, trophy, etc.)?
- Did you intervene in a situation that could have become a serious problem had you not detected it?
- Was your suggestion adopted by your classmates, team or coworkers?
- Did you accomplish a task using fewer resources than usual?
- Did you satisfy a particularly demanding client?
- Did you initiate something?
- Have you trained or taught people?[76]

Add your achievements to your career story and, when relevant, to your resume. Look for patterns in your achievements. This could help clarify longer-term career goals. For example, if your goal is to become a Vice President in a corporation and you have not managed a team yet, that is an achievement you'll have to attain. When reviewing your achievements, you may uncover a theme. For instance, you note that the majority of your achievements highlight your strategic capabilities. In that case, look for opportunities for bigger achievements in that area.

41
What are my educational attainments?

Educational attainments can be defined in two broad categories: credentialed and non-credentialed. Credentialed attainments are recognized degrees and certificates by validated institutions, such as Bachelor's, Master's and PhD degrees from universities. Non-credentialed education is knowledge attained that is not officially recognized. This could be a non-credit adult learning class, professional trade courses, or research and reading you've conducted on your own to learn about a topic.

A third category has been emerging–primarily through online learning–called "alternative credentials." These alternative credentials offer a way to verify your education attainment through a documented source that is not part of the traditional academic system. You can display alternative credentials on your resume to inform employers about your knowledge of specific skills and competencies. Examples of online offering are Coursera and Udemy edX, as well as online branches of well-known universities such as Duke, The New School, and Cornell.

According to Cathy Sandeen, non-degree certificates are usually recognized by employers:

> In my previous role as dean of UCLA Extension, one of the nation's largest providers of non-degree educational programs, we offered nearly 150 professional certificate programs that did not carry degree-level academic credit but were widely recognized by employers as complementing more traditional academic programs.[77]

When defining your academic achievements, include credentialed, non-credentialed, and alternative credential options. Today, as job requirements rapidly change, consider how you will continue your education.

Incorporate time in your schedule for perpetual learning and its documentation. Note your academic accomplishments on your resume, on LinkedIn, and in your career story.

Skills

There are two sets of skills acquired through education and experience: hard skills and soft skills. Understand the difference between them and their importance in each job. Identify the hard and soft skills you possess and which skills you need to improve.

42
What are "hard skills?"

Hard skills are referred to as "cognitive" skills as they involve an intellectual process. They are information-based, meaning they can be taught and learned in a consistent fashion, and are usually associated with a specific industry. These are the skills you've acquired on how to do XYZ, such as math, writing, driving a car, or using a word processing program.

There is an historical debate about the importance of hard skills vs. soft skills that reaches back to the early 1900s.

In 1918, Charles Riborg Mann, a physicist, engineer, and civilian adviser in the US War Department, published research that discussed the importance of soft skills versus hard skills in engineering disciplines. Mann's report concludes that soft skills contribute to the success of an engineer. Hard skills in a vacuum are not valuable. Their value is constituted in their delivery through soft skills.[78]

Let's use the role of a web designer as an example to look at some of the hard skills you would need:

- Basic math
- Color theory
- Typography
- Principles of a good layout
- Use of various computer software, like the Adobe suite of products
- Understanding of coding and platforms

These skills would be taught in a classroom, if you were studying web design. They are necessary for the job, but even if you perfected these hard skills, if you didn't have any soft skills—communication skills, empathy, and problem solving—you'd be a terrible web designer!

43
What are "soft skills?"

Soft skills are "non-cognitive" skills, the personality traits and behaviors that facilitate working in a business environment, many of which are influenced by your emotional intelligence. Essentially, they refer to how you work with people and manage situations. Soft skills include: communication, teamwork, creativity, problem solving, and reliability, to name a few.

Today, employers tend to emphasize soft skills because many hard skills have a short lifespan due to advances in technology and other factors.

> Skills and knowledge regeneration is constant and employees need to have the right mindset that enables them to keep learning, keep developing and keep moving forward...It's all about agility. It's a VUCA (volatile, uncertain, complex and ambiguous) world that we live and work in...Being agile requires employees to have a whole host of personal attributes that fall into the soft skills category—flexibility, adaptability, creativity, dynamism, connectedness, emotional intelligence and so it goes on.[79]

An article in Forbes noted four key soft skills sought after in millennials:

- **ATTENTION**—Ability to focus for the length of a project or task, detail-oriented perspective, and good time management. Not easily distracted.
- **MORE THAN COLLEGE**—Experience in the work world, managing people and working with colleagues and customers. (This can be attained through internships or part-time work during school.)

- **AGILITY**—Going beyond a specific expertise and changing with the situation or with the times. This is particularly relevant in startup culture.
- **HUMILITY**—Consciousness of what you don't know, the ability to acknowledge your limitations and ask for help.[80]

Although we can't predict what skills will be valued in ten years, the current trend shows a preference towards soft skills. "When evaluating who they will hire in 2017, 62 percent of employers rated the candidate's soft skills as very important (i.e., skills associated with one's personality such as positive attitude, team-oriented or dependable)."[81]

Even more highly valued are those who have both soft skills and analytical skills. "Employment in these hybrid occupations has grown 94% since 1980 (from 39 million to 76 million), representing a higher growth rate than jobs requiring higher social skills or those calling for higher analytical skills."[82]

As the knowledge industry evolves to include more artificial intelligence, robotics, and other computer-aided workforce support, the more "human" skills that cannot yet be mimicked by technology are more highly valued. The good news is that there are many ways to improve your soft skills which do not require a large investment.

Soft skills are not typically taught in universities as classes, but there are books, online classes, and other educational vehicles through which they can be learned or improved. However, the best way to learn them is through actual work experience. For example, it's difficult to know how to work under deadline pressure by reading about it! You could read about the approaches you should take—remaining calm, focusing, and prioritizing—but reading doesn't prepare you for the physicality of the event: an increase in heart rate, cranked up adrenaline, and possibly people yelling at you! That only happens when you are in the moment.

In a recent Pew Research survey, of the four top soft skills, only one was learned most often through formal education. The following shows what percentage of respondents think that these key soft skills are learned through formal education:

- Interpersonal Skills: 8%
- Management and Leadership: 8%
- Critical Thinking: 19%
- Written and Spoken Communication: 42%[83]

The majority thought these skills are learned through either life experience or on the job.

Most employers rank soft skills as important, but their job search process may not be designed to identify those with the best soft skills. The Wall Street Journal "conducted a survey of nearly 900 executives in 2015, [and] found 92% said soft skills were equally important or more important than technical skills. Yet, a big majority, 89%, said they have a very or somewhat difficult time finding people with the requisite attributes."[84]

Why the disconnect? Ryan Craig, in a TechCrunch article, hypothesizes that the automated, keyword-based system used by most companies is not triggered by soft skill keywords. That means the first cut in the process is not filtering properly for soft skills, but Craig foresees that a "shift to competency-based hiring is inevitable...to include candidates with great soft skills, and likely more diverse backgrounds than the current pedigree- and degree-based hiring system allows."[85]

Realize that soft skills are valued and evaluate which you excel in and which you need to improve. Consider optimizing these skills in an internship, part-time job, or volunteer position.

44

What is the most important skill anyone can have?

Although each role has its own key skills, being an active listener may be the most important skill across the board. The good news is that it's a skill anyone can acquire or improve.

What does active listening entail? An active listener comprehensively processes incoming verbal information, but is also perceptive of non-verbal communication. In his book, Michael Hope defines active listening as:

> ... a way of listening and responding to another person that improves mutual understanding...The listener must take care to attend to the speaker fully, and then repeats, in the listener's own words, what he or she thinks the speaker has said. The listener does not have to agree with the speaker; he or she must simply state what they think the speaker said.[86]

However, this is not the typical method we use to communicate. In fact, various studies have agreed that we remember only 25-50% of what we hear. According to an article by Sue Shellenbarger's in the Wall Street Journal, "The failure to listen well not only prolongs meetings and discussions but also can hurt relationships and damage careers."[87]

Then how can you become a better listener? It requires taking steps before and during a conversation. Following are some suggestions from Shellenbarger, (with my modifications) on what makes a better listener:

Before a conversation:

- Clear your mind through a brain dump—document all that is occupying your mind. You can follow through on these issues later.
- List questions or topics you want to cover. This will avoid wasting time trying to think of them in the moment.
- Limit the time you spend talking to about 25% of the conversation.
- Get rid of assumptions about what you expect the other person will say.
- Remove any distractions, which include family members/ friends, devices, and distracting environments (loud city streets or other active environments).

During the conversation:

- Take notes to stay focused while listening.
- At key moments, paraphrase what you think the speaker said and ask for their confirmation.
- Assure the discussion stays on track by asking clarifying questions when necessary.
- If meeting in person, read the speaker's body language and facial expressions for additional insights on their intention. If it's a phone call, gain insights by listening to intonation, pauses, and emphasis of voice.
- Use pauses to reflect or draw out more information.

Your Professional Brand

Your professional brand is derived from the five dimensions of self-awareness and encapsulates your identity so that employers can understand your value. To define your professional brand, you'll go through a step-by-step process resulting in the marketing materials you'll need to engage with potential employers.

45

What is a "professional brand," and why do I need one?

What is it?

The concept of a "professional brand" evolved from applying the practice of branding for businesses to the individual. Today, branding is a key component of representing yourself in your network and to potential employers. Through branding, you distinguish yourself from your colleagues and establish your professional value. It helps you clarify your contribution to an employer and allows for employers to decide on your suitability for a role.

What is the definition of branding?

Most simply stated, the goal of branding is to associate value with something: a person, product, service, or company. The perceived value of the brand drives the actual worth. How much a car costs, what you pay for dinner in a restaurant, the job title you are given, and how much you're paid are all impacted by the brand values expressed.

How is your professional brand defined?

Your brand grows from the authentic kernel of you, what makes you unique. Only you can define your professional brand—it is the culmination of your self-awareness.

What determines the success of your professional brand?

Your brand's success is determined by the feedback of your employer/network. The feedback component ensures the authenticity of what your brand is claiming. If you claim you are an expert at writing copy for social media channels, but your client receives no response from the work you've done, you lose authenticity. If you position yourself as an innovative designer but deliver a website design that looks like a Microsoft Word template, you will lose credibility. In this way, the success of your brand in the marketplace validates it.

Why do I need it?

Although one of the goals of this book is to take you through the process of searching for and landing a job, the ideal scenario is not searching for a job! Your goal is to have employers seek you out and fight over you! If you build a successful brand, employers will find you—you won't have to look for them. With a well-defined professional brand comes:

- **LOYALTY**—a trustworthy following; a supportive network
- **AUTHORITY**—power to influence or command thought, opinion, or behavior
- **VALIDITY**—well-grounded or justifiable claims; being relevant and meaningful

Expressing your brand

The following is inspired by Susan Solomon's perspective on business branding:

> Today, your professional brand is expressed through your physical presence and actions as well as the "online you"—your social media presence. Most likely, the online you will precede a meeting with the physical you. That's why it's so important to manage your online presence. Ensure the physical you aligns with your social media presence. (That means current photos in your LinkedIn profile!) The physical you includes how you speak, your tone of voice, your handshake and the "vibe" people get from you. You can't change many of these attributes, but you should be conscious of what they are and how people respond to them.[88]

Content that is posted online, by you and others who write about you, is accessible for everyone to see. It could be your profile on LinkedIn, your tweets, or getting tagged in someone else's Facebook post. In addition to social media content, there's content distributed by word of mouth from friends, family, professors, coworkers, and others.

Finally, there is your behavior—what you do and how you do it. How hard do you work? Are you a leader? Do you work well with others? Do you manage challenging situations? Your actions go a long way in influencing how you are remembered.

Presence, content and behavior combine to represent you and form your brand, and it is up to you to manage it. Susan Solomon suggests considering these questions about brand management:

- What will public content communicate about you?
- What's your attitude and personality? Are you funny? Understanding? Sophisticated?
- What is your appearance? How do you dress? Follow the status quo, cool, fashionably or conservatively?
- How do you speak? A thousand words a minute or carefully measuring each word?
- What is your career story? What is the narrative of your career that has brought you to this point in time?
- What are your posts about? What are your friends and associates posting about you?[89]

Your professional brand is the framework for how you look, sound, feel, and behave. It's encountered in every experience people have with the real or virtual you.

Without a clear brand foundation, making the right choices about how and what to communicate is fraught with complications. You may know who you are, but without an actionable framework for your professional brand, your time and efforts in defining yourself, building your network, and seeking the right job for you won't be communicated. That's the long answer to why brand matters!

46
How do I build my professional brand?

There is a specific process for building a professional brand. Start by building the brand framework, as described below. Your brand will continue to evolve over the life of your career. Your brand is composed of four components: Identity, Expression, Experiences, and Amplification. Let's review each component.

Identity

Brand building starts with an exploration of your identity. After you've gained a sense of self-awareness, define your professional identity in a way that can be comprehensively expressed to your colleagues and employers. Consider both your characteristics and the services you offer—the "package" you offer in exchange for a salary.

Create a document, following the one below as a template. This document is for your eyes only and serves as the framework for the other three components. For this example, I'm using a software developer whose unique strength is her communication ability:

Keywords

Identify three keywords or keyword phrases that describe the "what" and "how" of you. The "what" is your expertise—the combination of your skills, knowledge, and experience. The "how" is the delivery of the "what." Imagine you are creating an ad for yourself online; what keywords would someone enter in a search engine to find you? Consider how people respond to you, how you make them feel.

Choose the three words carefully. They should be "loaded" with multiple relevant meanings. For example, I could say I am innovative, a self-starter, and a leader, but if I said I was entrepreneurial, that would imply those three words. Avoid simple adjectives like "great." Start with a long list of words, and narrow it down. Use a thesaurus, and most importantly, ask colleagues who know you well for input.

These three words represent the distilled version of you and the essence of your brand. They will provide the foundation for your marketing materials, define how you interact with people—both online and in person—and serve as your "North Star" when making career decisions.

For our developer, her keyword phrases are: app development master, inspirational, customer-centric communicator.

Mission

Think about the practical answer to the questions: What does my professional brand do? Who does it do it for? How does it do it? Your mission statement can be used on your business card, be the lead sentence for the Summary section of your LinkedIn profile, and serve as the basis of your job pitch. Our example developer used her mission statement as the opening sentence for her LinkedIn Summary: Masterful and inspirational developer with customer-centric communication skills who contributes to teams building industry-leading apps.

Your mission may change from job to job. When crafting it, consider what you can accomplish for your employer in your next role. Imagine you're in a line-up with nine other people with your qualifications; what would make you unique as compared to the competition?

Uniqueness is typically bred from combinations of your interests and abilities. In our developer example, her talent and interest in writing make her a good communicator and a stand-out in her role. Typically, developers are not known for their communication abilities, so that soft skill distinguishes her and drives up her value.

Vision

Write a short, memorable, inspirational statement defining the optimal future state of your professional brand, one that will endure over time. Defining a vision is important because if you just go from job to job without a career vision, you are not managing your career path. Bring a conscious purpose to each job you take. Use your past to imagine your future. Work backwards from your ideal end state—your ultimate job—to figure out the next step in your timeline. Going back to our developer example, her vision would be, "Convert the dreams of customers into technological solutions that change the way the world does business."

Expression

The three dimensions above are the foundation for how your professional brand becomes a reality. Once it is defined, you can express it to others through the following three mediums.

Physical Presence

How you dress, your style, your physicality, your voice, your "vibe," and your way of speaking and walking all make up your physical presence. Your physical presence makes an impression on people in the same way that the package impacts the attractiveness of a product on a shelf. Are you presenting yourself in the best package possible? Examine how people react to you. Objectively watch yourself on video, and note what you'd like to modify.

Digital Presence

Your digital presence is revealed when someone finds you through an online search, or through social media channels like LinkedIn, Facebook, and Twitter. It includes your posts and posts made by others about you. Ideally, there shouldn't be any surprises that reflect negatively on your brand. It's likely most people will "meet" you online before they meet you in person.

The commonality of your name will impact your digital presence. There are likely several 'Jane Jones' living in New York City. It's up to you to try to distinguish yourself if your name is common. Since LinkedIn has a high ranking in Google searches, first try to ensure you are the top profile for your name on LinkedIn. Complete your profile, publish articles, list skills and keywords throughout your profile.

Marketing Materials

Marketing materials are any printed or digital materials created by you to promote your brand and engage potential employers. These materials follow essentially the same principles as marketing materials for a company, product, or service. There are two components: visual identity and content.

- **VISUAL IDENTITY**—The visual components that express your professional brand in marketing materials, include color palette, logo, fonts, photography/illustration style, and style choices for print, online, and other support materials. For example, our developer would use cool colors and modern sans serif fonts to represent her professional brand.
- **CONTENT & VOICE**—This is the copywriting of your marketing materials. It is the words and messages, and the way in which you say them—the voice. Do you sound authoritative, approachable, or conservative? Your voice is reflected in the About section on your website, your pitch, and in your "thank you" card. It should be consistent and recognizably you.

Individual marketing items will vary depending on your industry, but a few consistent elements are:

- Gmail email address with your name
- Business card
- Resume
- Pitch
- LinkedIn Profile
- Thank you note card

If you're a freelancer or small business owner, add one or more of these materials as well:

- Website
- Portfolio
- Blog
- Social Media
- Tagline
- Stationery & Envelope

- Promotional product (a leave behind with your business name: postcard, pen, mug, etc.)

Experiences

Experiences are what happens when your professional brand interacts with the world. It includes your career achievements, interactions with supervisors and coworkers, leadership activities, philanthropic activities, and educational attainments. These experiences will provide the basis of your career story.

Amplification

Amplification is the communication of your recorded experiences through the proper channels. If you do a great job, but no one knows about it, you haven't produced the proper impact with your efforts. Speak about your experiences, not to brag, but from a place of imparting value. Examples of amplification include announcing a career achievement in your alumni magazine, writing an article based on your expertise on LinkedIn, or presenting at an industry conference on Twitter. Consider what channels are favored in your industry.

Keep it real

Building a brand is no easy feat, but if you work from a place of authenticity and consistency, positive results will be seen over time.

Network & Relationships

After getting to know yourself, as we examined in the sections on self-awareness, the next most important part of a successful career is the relationships you build with colleagues, employers/clients, vendors, mentors, and mentees. Networking and business relationships have always been key drivers in business success. "Networking is the single most powerful marketing tactic to accelerate and sustain success for any individual or organization!" [90]

In today's marketplace, you simply cannot be successful without the support of others. When there's a job opening, most everyone reviews their list of contacts before formally posting a job. The better connected you are, the more likely you'll be contacted first.

The key to relationships in business, as in your personal life, is to be authentic. While you should be respectful of everyone you encounter, you are not going to engage in long-term business relationships with everyone, and that is okay.

47

What is a network and networking?

A network is a contact list of people you keep track of throughout your career. Your network should be actively managed. That means ensuring you contact people at regular intervals (how often depends on your connection with them) to check in and find out how you can be of help. It also means seeking out connections with new people.

How do you meet new people? That is where networking comes into play. Networking is the act of meeting people with whom you can form a relationship that is mutually beneficial. The benefit may be in meeting an immediate need, such as finding a job or hiring for a role. You might be new to an industry or to a location, and you're looking to get support from those who know more than you.

Networking can occur anywhere—from the formalized setting of a planned networking event to a casual coffee between two coworkers. Networking will happen in both conscious and in unplanned ways. For intentional networking, you may attend networking events held by your college, fellow interns, past colleagues, industry groups, or local organizations that promote business. Alternatively, you may be randomly contacted by a friend who thinks someone may be a good contact for you, or you may meet someone online and realize you both work in the same industry.

Following are insights on networking from Luke who runs several networking events.

> "Networking" gets a bad name because there are people who aren't very giving and are just out for themselves. I've found over and over that by offering a lot of help, others help me too. (Pay it forward and/or directly from people I've helped.)

Ideally people are sincerely offering help vs. saying they will and not following through.

Follow-through is my big pet peeve—people don't do it enough, even when it's helping them. For example, I'll meet a job-searcher and mention four people who could help them in their search and the person never responds.

From a logistics standpoint, it seems a lot of networking happens in one-on-one sessions over coffee/drinks, the phone, Skype, etc. If it's two people who know one another quite well, they often don't even call it networking.

There are networking events where people meet over drinks/breakfast or in groups, or even trade shows. This is a different than the one-on-one sessions. I find that to build a relationship from those larger groups entails a meeting of two or three others after the initial event.

Finally, I know people who get a lot out of "Mastermind" sessions, where people brainstorm on one another's behalf. This seems to be smaller groups (4-12 people) who get to know one another well over time.[91]

What networking comes down to is one thing: do you like each other? When you have the choice, you want to work with people that you like. Let's face it, you spend most of your day with coworkers!

"Membership" levels

Just like a membership to a museum or organization, your network will include several levels, or more accurately, concentric circles:

- **CONTACT**—This is someone you met or have done business with, most likely a "one-off" interaction. You will remember at least one aspect of your meeting—the conditions of your meeting, their name, or their face—but not much more.

- **MEMBER**—You know everyone in this group by name and face because you have worked with them or had other interactions.
- **BOARD**—This small group of people are those whose opinions you trust, from whom you solicit advice and connections, and who have been demonstrably supportive of you.

Network management is the formal and conscious development of business relationships for mutual support. It is a two-way street; you ask for support, and you give it, but don't expect it to always be an even exchange.

48
How do I start my network?

Launch your network by adding your current contacts. Extend the boundaries of your family and friends network as many levels deep as you can. With "six degrees of separation," you could theoretically reach anyone in the world through your network! It's easier to start networking with people you know because you'll feel more comfortable asking them for support.

If you have a very small network to start, don't be discouraged. Following are some methods for expanding your network from Jeremy:

- Start with who you know — your family, your family friends, your college friends, your neighbors, and anyone already part of an existing professional network, such as from internships or summer jobs.
- Ask your network if there are industries or companies you should be researching.
- When you connect with a new contact, ask if there are other people you should be talking with. You aren't asking for a job; you're asking for information that might help you find the right industry, role, or company.[92]

Build on the relationships you form, starting in college, and continue as you evolve your career. Your schoolmates and colleagues are the backbone of your network. As you move into each new job, you'll develop a new cluster of contacts for your network. Stay in touch, and help each other. Enjoy the entire process of networking. If you are not enjoying it, it will come across to others and hamper your ability to grow.

49

How can my network help me in my career?

Your network is your secret weapon for attaining information and connections that you could not achieve on your own. Are you looking for a job or an informational interview? Are you trying to learn more about a company or more about the experience of a specific role? Ask your network.

Before asking for help from someone in your network, be 100% clear about what you're requesting. The clearer you are, the better the response will be. I frequently receive requests that read, "Do you know any designers?" That's it! That question is too broad. It then puts the burden on me to ask more questions: What type of designers? Full-time or project-based? What compensation is being offered? What level of experience? Try to imagine what questions someone might have, and address as many of them as possible in the first contact.

What mode of contact should you use? Presume that email is best. That will allow the recipient to respond at a time that works best for them. Email also makes it easier for your contact to forward your request to others, if necessary. Don't be afraid to follow up. A week's time is fair.

Be sure you have something to offer your contact. That could be as simple as suggesting an article of interest, a quote from a seminar you attended, or an announcement about an upcoming event in their industry.

Today, almost 80% of the jobs found will be through networking.[93] It's definitely not through just posting a resume online! Online sites have created a false sense of being proactive. It's all about your network and the relationships you build. Over time, that's how your career will progress.

When I started out, I landed my first job through my family. I told my Aunt Bessie that I was looking for a job as a graphic designer, preferably in-house for a corporation. My aunt worked at an insurance company but didn't know of any openings. She mentioned it to the concierge in her office building, and he knew a printer in the building whose client was an insurance conglomerate. The printer knew someone in a newly formed branch of the company who was looking for a graphic designer! It was a very circuitous route, but this is commonly how jobs are found.

50

How do I manage my network?

Managing your professional network is comprised of two components. First, there is the digital storage of your contacts and the addition of new contacts to whatever system you are using. Second, is the ways by which you ensure your network stays relevant to you and you stay relevant to those in your network.

Today, most people use the online social network, LinkedIn, to house contacts. LinkedIn is by far the most popular professional social media network.

It's a good practice to also keep a copy of your contacts in a contact database such as Contacts on iOS or Android. You can either enter your contacts into your contact database, and then import them into LinkedIn, or visa-versa. If you enter them into your contact database first, sort your contacts into groups. Using groups helps categorize your contacts to help you find them more easily. For example, your groups might be:

- Colleagues
- Prospective Employers
- Clients
- Vendors
- Freelancers

Consider how you will enter your contacts. Although there are apps that help facilitate the process, the simplest option may be to:

1   Create a business contact entry for yourself in the contact app on your mobile device. Include your phone number and social media contacts you use for business such as LinkedIn and Twitter.
2   When you meet someone in person, share your professional contact info through your contact app.

3   If you make new contacts online, use an app or service that pulls the contact info from email signatures, or enter it manually into your contact app. If you go to trade shows and conferences where business cards are used, get a business card scanner to input all the new contacts.

4   Import your contacts into LinkedIn. Also, export your contacts every few months from LinkedIn to ensure you have a back-up.

Luke, who runs a professional networking event, has the following advice on managing your network:

Follow up

One easy thing is to be very disciplined about connecting with people on LinkedIn after meeting, and making sure to connect with classmates, friends, and acquaintances. It's best to connect with people you've met face to face or on the phone. When meeting new people, ask for two to four referrals of other people they could introduce to you.

Start something

Another idea is to pick an area you're interested in (professionally or otherwise) and just invite folks to join a group and/or attend events. Be the organizer, and you'll become the nexus of people and connections which allows you to be perceived as a leader. The more you can leverage those connections to help others, the more connections and positive feedback will be returned to you.

Some thoughts about the first couple events you host:

1   **SEED THE MARKET**—Start by running your proposed date/place by at least three or four people so that

even if it's only that small group, it's worth it for those people.

2 **EXPAND THE GROUP**—Once you have commitment from the first group, invite a few others. Where possible, reference the background/experience/awesomeness of those who have already committed.

3 **SPREAD THE WORD**—Go to other events to tell them about yours. Invite a mix of people—some more networky, some better at follow-up, some with more time, and some that know more people, etc.[94]

51

How do I expand my network?

Join professional organizations

A great way to extend your network is to join professional organizations. Some organizations require fees for joining, others charge by the event. Some have a combination of both. Large companies, depending on their policies, may cover the fees for your professional organization membership. If you are not employed by a company who will pay the fees, set a budget for the annual fees and select organizations accordingly. Be sure to join the most highly recognized organizations in your field. Through these organizations, you will stay in the know about the latest trends in your field. You will also make connections that will help further your career.

Corporations and corporate networks

Working for a large, global corporation exposes you to many people who could become part of your network. Most large corporations provide affinity networks for different groups or causes. For example, when I worked for a large financial corporation, there were fourteen affinity networks ranging from LGBTQ to religion-focused. These groups allow for additional networking, leadership opportunities, and chances to try new skills.

Cross-industry events

In addition to making connections within your industry, it's also important to get info from outside of your industry if you want to have a 360-degree view of what's happening in the world. Attend group meetings or any other events of interest, and join online groups in LinkedIn and MeetUps. What makes you unique is your expertise combined with your other interests.

Admired brands

The ideal company to work for is one that you already admire and that is world renowned! If you love their products or services, it will make you feel great to work there. Write down the products and services you love and try searching for those companies on LinkedIn and Glassdoor.com to learn more about them. Connect with employees at those companies through LinkedIn. Start your introductions by telling them how much you love the brand. Keep in mind, when you work for successful, globally recognized brands, you benefit from a halo effect that positively impacts your brand!

52
How do I prepare for a networking event?

Prepare before you attend a networking event. Follow these steps:

1 Review the list of attendees, if available.
2 Unless otherwise specifically noted, attire should be "business"—whatever that means in your industry. For a real estate agent, that means a suit and tie. For a software developer, that means jeans and a "nice" shirt.
3 Bring as many business cards as you could possibly distribute during the time you are attending. Assuming you are busily networking, that would mean five minutes per person, or twelve people per hour.
4 Practice your pitch. Make sure you have your pitch down cold.
5 Be prepared to take notes that will help you remember who your new contacts are and where you met. Use the method most comfortable for you. That may mean bringing a pen and small pad, making notes on business cards, or entering new contacts into your phone with a notation.

Nelly has run a professional networking group for many years and provides us with the following advice:

Make sure that you have a specific, articulable, and perhaps even measurable goal in mind when going to a networking event. This requires a careful assessment of what you need at the time and the type or category of professional you want to fulfill your need. Look through who will be in attendance, determine if there are specific types of professionals who will attend, even identify specific people that you would like to meet before you go. If there are some specific people that you would like to meet, find out more about them through their social media efforts and other vehicles, identify commonality between you both and that will help you make an instant connection.

When you run into a conversation that isn't in keeping with your goals, regardless of how pleasant it is, you will need to somehow, politely, extricate yourself from that conversation and continue in your quest to achieve your goals for the event. Upon achieving your goals, you can always go back and reconnect with the person with whom you were enjoying your conversation and pick where you left off.[95]

53

What makes a networking event successful?

Your goal at any networking event is to meet as many "qualified" people as possible. "Qualified" means someone who fits your criteria: they align with you on values, you like them, and you can potentially support each other. Remember, everyone will have the same objective. Following are key steps to follow at the event:

1 Be authentic.
2 Be clear on your goals. Some options are:
   - Find a new job or project
   - Expand your network
   - Fill a role for a colleague
   - Hire for a current or future role
3 Start a conversation with an introduction, then a question. For example, "Hi" (if they are alone) or "Excuse me" (if they are part of a group). "I'm (First Name, Last Name), and I (description of your job). Have you been to this event before?"
4 Assess what your business relationship might be:
   - **INSIDE AGENT**—same role and industry, different companies
   - **ALLY**—different roles, same company
   - **MIND EXPANDER**—different enough roles that you can learn about something new that will add depth to your expertise
   - **MENTOR**—in a supervisory role to you, or someone with more work experience, a source of advice
   - **MENTEE**—in a less experienced role than you who would benefit from your advice
5 Excuse yourself after you know enough to complete step 4. Find a pause, and mention how much you enjoyed the meeting, then

offer your business card. Depending on your assessment of the situation, determine your next steps.

- If there is an immediate opportunity, suggest scheduling a meeting.
- If you'd like to stay in touch, mention that you will send an invitation from LinkedIn. Be in touch the next day.
- If you don't expect to stay in touch, leave it at that.

Many people don't like networking because they feel like they are just 'taking' from others. If that's how you feel, try sending your new contact an article or a link to something that you discussed during your conversation or that you thought they might be interested in. That lets them know you were thinking about what you can do for them as well as how they can help you. It's a small gesture, but can be an effective way to keep the connection going.

6 Connect people within the event. For example, if you met someone who was looking for a developer, then you meet a developer, connect the two people. This will put you in good standing with both and may be communicated to others at the event.

7 If alcohol is available, limit your consumption! The last thing you want to do is impair your brand.

Nelly summarized what makes a networking event successful, based on her extensive networking experience:

Intention makes a networking event successful. The responsibility for making a networking event successful lies squarely on the shoulders of the attendee. Do your homework, prepare yourself, plan it out, and stick to your plan...with flexibility.

Remember though, that others have goals too and you might be the perfect person that someone else is looking to connect with, so also be prepared to listen and be helpful. You never know who that person knows and who that person might be able to connect you with...that is the magic of networking.

Creating the right mindset for connecting with the people that you need to connect with makes it successful. Being prepared makes it successful. Knowing who you are and being able to articulate what you need in a manner that is compelling makes it successful. Ensuring that you don't get mired down in a conversation that isn't productive makes it successful.[96]

54
What if I don't like networking?

Attending networking events can be stressful—sometimes for some people, and all the time for other people—but it shouldn't be! You don't have to be a "party person" or an extrovert to be successful at networking events. Keep in mind that you are valuable to others. Your objective at the networking event is to introduce yourself to as many people as possible. Enjoy it!

You may initially find networking difficult for one of more of the following reasons:

- **CHALLENGES WITH PUBLIC SPEAKING**—Even though you are not literally on a stage, you may feel you are in the spotlight when introducing yourself.
- **FEAR OF REJECTION**—What if someone walks away after you introduce yourself, or you're ignored when trying to introduce yourself to a group?
- **LACK OF CONFIDENCE**—If you don't have your pitch memorized, or are otherwise unprepared, that could affect your level of confidence.

How do you overcome these issues?

- **PRACTICE PUBLIC SPEAKING**—Start by presenting your pitch in front of a mirror. Then, video tape yourself with your smartphone. Play it back, and try to objectively assess how you come across. Is your voice too soft? Are you fidgeting? Do you say "um" or other filler word too much? Do you "look" professional and confident? Are you interested in what you are saying?

Once you've practiced a few times, try it in front of friends or colleagues.

■ **NOT EVERYONE IS GOING TO BE A CONNECTION**—Don't take it personally. If you are not in a receptive group, move on! And remember to have fun! Most people will sense your positivity and will respond with like energy.

55
Are business cards relevant?

The answer to this FAQ is—to my surprise—yes, for most industries. I thought that digital cards or other innovation would have taken over long ago, but it hasn't happened. There is something valuable in the tradition, almost like trading gifts. Having something tactile and tangible as a reminder of your meeting makes it more real.

Even when you're not networking per se, carry your business cards. A business opportunity can happen anywhere! There doesn't have to be an immediate opportunity, either, for it to be worth cultivating a new contact. In fact, it usually doesn't work that way. You are building a relationship for the future.

Designing your business card

Design an impressive business card, and think of it as a promotional item. Make something memorable that will make the recipient pause when looking through a stack of business cards.

Structurally, use the front and back. Choose a paper that has weight and is reflective of your brand. There are essentially two types of paper, coated and uncoated. There are several variations on each. New, thicker papers offer a colored edge. Hire a great printer, and ask to see samples.

The design should reflect your brand through color, fonts, graphics, textures, and emotional impact. Elements should be laid out with enough white space, and be organized to emphasize the right information.

You can hire a designer, if you have the budget, or work with an online service that offers high quality templates. You can also research what others in your industry do by attending an industry-specific networking event and collecting business cards.

Content-wise, the minimal info you should have on your business card is:

- Name
- Email
- Mobile Phone

- Website and/or Social Media

If you're in a creative field, you can also include:

- Work sample
- Portfolio website

If you choose to include a work sample, you can make a consistent card, or mix it up so that each card has a unique work sample.

Other items you can consider, if relevant in your industry:

- Your job title (e.g. Digital Marketing Expert or Illustrator)
- A quote from you or a famous person in your industry
- A tagline, which could be derived from your values
- List key clients or employers
- Your logo (if you have one for your professional brand)
- Blank space to allow you (or the recipient) to add customized notes based on the situation.

You may also choose to alter the card itself to make it distinctive:

- Die-cut cards which have a unique shape or non-standard size. (The standard 3.5" x 2" is best, as smaller cards get lost.)
- Letterpress cards (a more expensive printing process associated with high quality)
- Innovative uses of rubber stamps
- Various finishes: UV coating (ultra-shiny) or foils (metallic)

What you don't need:

- A physical address
- A list of all of your social media accounts

56
What is relationship building?

Through the experience of being in business, you will meet new people. As is the case in personal relationships, conscious effort and attention is required to build successful relationships. What does that entail? There are three essential steps:

Identify
Who is the person? Do you connect to them? What role would you each play in the relationship?

Connect
What is the best means for connecting (in person, by phone, by email, a combination, etc.)? How often should you be in touch? Do you meet up in groups or individually? Who else do you both know? Are there other people that you can connect each other to?

Appreciate
The "inner circle" of your network should be kept top of mind. Send them articles of interest, congratulate them on achievements, comment on articles they write, etc. Show your appreciation for everything they do for you.

Relationship building is valuable whether you have a full-time job or are a freelancer. In a full-time job, you will build relationships primarily with coworkers. As a freelancer, your relationships will be with clients.

Jeremy is an entrepreneur who has built two successfully companies. The success of his companies required numerous clients who he acquired through his excellent relationship building skills. Let hear what advice he has on relationship building:

Professional relationships, like personal relationships, are built on trust and give and take.

Trust is built over time—with consistent interactions that meet or exceed expectations. If you're just getting to know someone, you can start the process of building trust by nailing the small things: if you say you'll follow up tomorrow, aim to do it today. Consistency obviously requires multiple interactions. When building a relationship, find ways to offer value or be in touch periodically.

Give and take is a little trickier if you're just starting out in the workforce. It's likely that you'll be asking for help more than being able to provide help. But all hope is not lost—you can provide value in small ways: if someone recommends something to read, report your feedback. Give updates about your progress or your current thinking. Send a related article that you found interesting about a topic you've discussed in the past or a new company you've come across.[97]

57
What are the various relationship types?

In the business world, we experience many types of relationships that can contribute to our success. Below are descriptions of some key relationships:

- **MENTOR**—Someone, inside or outside of your industry, that has more experience and knowledge than you in specific areas where you need support.
- **ADVOCATE**—A colleague within your company that advocates for your advancement.
- **ROLE MODEL**—A public figure who inspires you. He or she does not have to be in your industry, but exhibits some behavior to which you aspire.

In today's complex and competitive job market, we need all three to advance, particularly in global corporations.

58

Why do I need a mentor, and how do I find one?

According to Merriam-Webster dictionary, a mentor is: "A trusted counselor or guide."[98]

A mentor offers good advice that makes you think and then come to your own decisions. The advice covers various aspects of your career. You may have a mentor who is more experienced than you in your exact role. Or, you may have a mentor that is an expert in HR and helps you prepare for a job search. Your mentor(s) can change over time as do other relationships. Your career trajectory may change leading you to seek guidance in a new subject matter. You may move up the ranks quickly and need more senior mentors.

How is the mentor-mentee relationship formed? Usually, in one of two ways. It can be casual—that is, you meet each other in another context and the relationship is formed. On the other hand, it can be a formal arrangement available through a school program, a job, or a professional organization. Formal programs will require that you fill out a form to help in the matching process.

Even if you're just starting out, it's great to take the role of a mentor as well. There is always someone who is more junior that could use the support. Start with your college or non-profits you admire.

59
What is an advocate?

In corporations, particularly at senior levels, advancement is supported through advocates. Advocates are peers or those with seniority who support your advancement.

Advocates can operate outside of corporate structures by providing support—strategic, emotional, or financial—as you advance through your career path. They can also function within the official organization to advance your career. In either case, the relationship can form informally or through a request by either party.

60
What's the value of a public figure as a role model?

What is the value of the career story of someone you don't personally know? A public figure can offer inspiration through their career story. I'll highlight two people that have inspired me.

Dyan Nyad is a swimmer who at the age of 64, after five failed attempts over 35 years, achieved her goal of swimming from Key West Florida to Cuba. She was the first person to do so without a shark cage. Dyan was eight-years-old when she first dreamed about making the 103-mile swim.

Louise Nevelson was an artist whose art broke into the male-dominated abstract expressionist movement (1940s through1960s). Although she knew she wanted to be an artist from age nine, public recognition for her work didn't come until she was in her 40s. Today, her work is in the Whitney, MOMA, and many other museums and exhibits internationally. Louise's insight should inspire us all: "...if you know what you have, then you know that there's nobody on earth that can affect you."[99]

These stories inspire me because of the unbreakable perseverance and strong self-awareness of these women. They battled both personal challenges and obstacles from the outside world. Both women were creative in their own ways and crushed conventional barriers.

Before you think about what the narrative of your career will be, can you think of anyone who has inspired you and why? Look for inspiration from positive stories in the media, in your circle of friends, and in your family.

Intelligence Gathering

We started "How do I cultivate my career?" by evaluating your self-awareness. Next, you examined how relationships with others is critical to your career success. Now, we'll focus on understanding the companies that will hire us, the parameters of industries, and the social, political, and economic global trends that affect us all. This investigation will prepare you for "The Job Search Life cycle."

I call this process "Intelligence Gathering," as opposed to "Research" or a similar name because finding information relevant to your career requires you to be a sleuth. You'll have to dredge through false information, conflicting information, and multiple sources.

Before we delve into the various tools and processes of intelligence gathering, let's assess the past and future states of work. We are on the cusp of what is being called the fourth revolution, The Knowledge Age, which has the potential to change life as we know it.

According to a January 2016 World Economic Forum report on the future of jobs:

> Disruptive changes to business models will have a profound impact on the employment landscape...ranging from significant job creation to job displacement, and from heightened labour productivity to widening skills gaps...By one popular estimate, 65% of children entering primary school today will ultimately end up working in completely new job types that don't yet exist.[100]

Changes more significant than the evolution from analog to digital are in progress. Your success will depend on how well you assess the world around you, and how you ensure your unique expertise retains its value. This means being a discerning consumer of higher education and postgraduate training and strategically selecting your roles and employers to cultivate your career.

61
What is the definition and history of work?

Definition of work

A definition of work by Peter Frase provides better context than its dictionary counterpart. (Full disclosure: Mr. Frase is part of the "post-workists" movement—those who predict and/or promote the end of work.) According to him, work is comprised of three components: "the means by which the economy produces goods, the means by which people earn income, and an activity that lends meaning or purpose to many people's lives."[101]

Of the three components which we use to define work, the last component is the only one over which you have control. If your life's purpose is an activity that is meaningful to you, whether or not it is work, you'll be in the best possible position as the role of work evolves in society.

History of Work

The Guardian article by Andy Beckett, "Post-work: the radical idea of a world without jobs," highlights a compressed history of work, signals the death of work as we know it today, and presents some of the theories and prophesies of the post-work movement. First, Beckett reminds us that humans have not always held the same beliefs or implementations of work:

> ...contrary to conventional wisdom, the work ideology is neither natural nor very old. "Work as we know it is a recent construct," says Hunnicutt. Like most historians, he identifies the main building blocks of our work culture as 16th-century Protestantism, which saw effortful labour as leading to a good afterlife; 19th-century industrial capitalism, which required disciplined workers and driven entrepreneurs; and the 20th-century desires for consumer goods and self-fulfillment.

The emergence of the modern work ethic from this chain of phenomena was "an accident of history," Hunnicutt says. Before then, "All cultures thought of work as a means to an end, not an end in itself." From urban ancient Greece to agrarian societies, work was either something to be outsourced to others—often slaves—or something to be done as quickly as possible so that the rest of life could happen.[102]

Our culture of work today in the United States values people who are too busy/important because they are always working, who sleep only three hours a night, and who earn big salaries in their jobs! However, underneath it all, isn't our goal the same as "urban Ancient Greece" and "agrarian societies:" outsource labor (as suggested by Timothy Ferriss in the successful book, *4-Hour Workweek)*, and live life by saving money to retire as early as possible and follow our passion?

62
What is the future of work?

These are all very deep and complex issues that are not meant to be resolved in the few paragraphs below. The intent of this FAQ is to suggest that you consider your career goals against the social, political, and economic evolution of work. Please do further research on this fascinating topic that will likely take dramatic twists and turns throughout your career.

What the future holds for work in our society is not clear. Many are now questioning if our current incarnation of work can continue due to many converging factors. Experts in this field hypothesize several scenarios; following are three examples:

1   A Universal Basic Income (UBI) for the majority of citizens—a base income received without working—which continues the current structures of capitalism and consumerism.
2   The end of labor and capitalism as we know it, which leads to a golden age of creativity for humanity.
3   An extreme state of poverty relegating the majority of the population to slavery, while the uber wealthy preside.

What is leading us to these outcomes? Several factors are converging. How each of these tracks progresses, and how businesses, government, and citizens respond will likely form work's destiny.

First up is the wealth gap which has "...really skyrocketed since about the 1980s." For example, "in the New York metro area, the 95th percentile makes $282,000 and the 20th percentile makes $23,000. These gaps between the rich and the poor in income and wealth are vast across the country and even worse in our cities."[103]

Overall, the position of the U.S. as a country of equitably distributed wealth has declined. "The CIA Factbook GINI index ranks the US as the

40th most unequal country in the world, below Ukraine, Bangladesh and Iran."[104] That is not a status to be proud of. Unfortunately, there is a potential for further decline in economic equality. This may impact where you want to live and work.

A common myth perpetuated in the U.S. is the "rags to riches" story which claims that anyone can achieve great power and wealth if they so desire, no matter how humble their background. This is not the reality. As explained to us by a financial advisor for high net worth individuals,

> [i]t is very difficult to create a net worth in excess of $10M from income alone. Yes, sports stars, entertainers, and some business people do — but they are rare. Those with a higher net worth tend to acquire most of their net worth from capital gains, not income that has been saved and invested. Large capital gains tend to come when private businesses are acquired by private or public companies with stock or when executives are paid directly by options or stock.[105]

He goes on to explain that the current system is unlikely to change as it is deeply entrenched in our society and tightly controlled by a small number of those with extreme wealth.

> A highly complex set of laws and exemptions from laws and taxes has been put in place by those in the uppermost reaches of the U.S. financial system. It allows them to protect and increase their wealth and significantly affect the U.S. political and legislative processes...Ordinary citizens in the bottom 99.9% ...have little likelihood of entering the top 0.5%, much less the top 0.1%. Moreover, those at the very top have no incentive whatsoever for revealing or changing the rules.[106]

This is not meant to be discouraging. On the contrary, knowing the reality of the situation is meant to be empowering. You may not acquire an excess of $10M during your career, but that doesn't mean you can't be happy and successful. This is the honest picture of what is attainable.

The second factor is the influence of climate change which has become a politicized topic because wealth and power are at stake. Traditional industries that have profited from the destruction of our planet and contributed to climate change are still holding on and promoting misinformation, but "[m]ake no mistake: climate catastrophes and extreme weather conditions, including cyclones, floods, drought, fires, melting glaciers, season changes, threats to agriculture and more, are increasing and impacting working people everywhere."[107] As one small example, "in the United States, Hurricane Sandy left 150,000 workers displaced and employment was overall reduced by 11,000 workers in New Jersey alone in 2012."[108]

That is just the tip of the iceberg. Climate change will likely impact the job market in the coming years. As I write this, the Caribbean is experiencing a succession of hurricanes, from Irma to Jose to Maria, which are devastating the entirety of Puerto Rico and throwing the regional economy into disarray.

And lastly, we must consider the long-term inevitability of automation and robotics as we progress from a blended workforce to an automated workforce. The future organization will have a new structure and new employees. The blended workforce is, and will continue to progress to be, composed of workers of various employment types—full-time, freelancers, consultants. A study exploring the gig economy found that "93% of companies already identify the blended workforce as they're seeing freelance workers teaming up with employees to work on projects together."[109]

The blending of different worker types will extend into automation. "[W]orkers are being augmented with machines and software. Together, these trends will result in the redesign of almost every job, as well as a new way of thinking about workforce planning and the nature of work."[110]

If we look at the jobs that employ the most people, many are automated already, at least to some degree, and others are in the process of automation: retail sales, cashiers, waiters/waitresses, janitorial staff. According to a McKinsey study, "almost every occupation has partial automation potential, as a significant percentage of its activities could be automated. We estimate that about half of all the activities people are paid to do in the worlds workforce could potentially be automated by adapting currently demonstrated technologies."[111]

Wow, that's worth emphasizing: half of all work executed today could be automated using technologies that exist today! (Let's also keep in mind that the source of this information is a management consulting company that would benefit from assisting companies in implementing this far-reaching automation.) That means that what is inhibiting a faster pace of business could have nothing to do with technological innovation, but may be hampered by the bureaucracies of large organizations or other systemic impediments. That could make this automation process take longer than predicted.

However, a more radical prediction is posed by Kevin Drum in an article for Mother Jones. He describes the progress being made in AI, which evolves exponentially fast, and predicts that we will reach full human level AI by 2045, within our lifetime:

> Around 2025 we'll finally start to see visible progress toward artificial intelligence. A decade later we'll be up to about one-tenth the power of a human brain, and a decade after that we'll have full human-level AI. It will seem like it happened overnight, but it's really the result of a century of steady—but mostly imperceptible—progress.[112]

This will impact jobs differently, depending on whether they are routine or not and whether they are physical or cognitive. Routine jobs are lost to AI first, and non-routine cognitive jobs last. Following are examples of each category from Drum's article:

> Routine physical: digging ditches, driving trucks
> Routine cognitive: accounts-payable clerk, telephone sales
> Non-routine physical: short-order cook, home health aide
> Non-routine cognitive: teacher, doctor, CEO[113]

What does this mean? Ultimately, the loss of jobs due to AI will lead to mass unemployment and requires us to rethink the societal structure. "[T]he answer to the mass unemployment of the AI Revolution has to involve some kind of sweeping redistribution of income that decouples it from work. Or a total rethinking of what 'work' is. Or a total rethinking of what wealth is.[114]

Although there are a few people sounding the alarm—Elon Musk, Bill Gates, and Eric Schmidt of Google, to name a few—the AI Revolution is not getting the serious attention it deserves. Without consideration and planning, we could descend into one of the dystopian worlds portrayed in many sci-fi movies where humans fight for survival against AI (2001: A Space Odyssey), humans fight against the "machines" (Terminator), or humans are nothing more than batteries for the evil AI system (The Matrix).

How could the AI revolution result in a utopian society? If AI is successfully incorporated into our infrastructure, it would mean we do not have to spend our time working for an income. We could then theoretically evolve to a higher state of consciousness, above that of robots and AI, from which we can form a society where each person lives life to their fullest potential.

Against this backdrop, how do you manage your career today? Lean towards work in category four, non-routine cognitive, and stay informed on how this issue progresses while building your wealth!

On the other hand, the future of work could be inconsequential, if you are following the premise of this book. If you truly seek, experience, and contribute to what is most relevant to you, whether you are paid for what you do is irrelevant. We need to be aware of what the future might bring, but reality is in the present.

63

What is intelligence gathering?

Intelligence gathering is finding out information about jobs, companies, industries and global trends to help in defining your career goals and keep you informed about your industry. Before you make a commitment to a field of study or search for a job, conduct intelligence gathering to prove your assumptions and understand the current state of occupations, companies, industries, and global trends. Formulate your career in the context of these broad categories.

Today, as opposed to fifty years ago, there are a lot of tools to help you access this information, but there is also more information! Keeping up with this info is a task that requires its own strategy. Start by customizing the newsfeeds on your default news apps. If you're on a Mac platform, use the News app that comes with the mobile iOS. If you're on Android, News&Weather is the default app. There are many independent readers you could also use, depending on your needs and how extensively you want to customize the information delivered to you.

In our world of endless information, it's critical to ensure your information is from a valid source. Use many different channels to find the information you need. Check online for company research or research about the person who is going to interview you. Attend a conference, or schedule an informational meeting with an employee at a company you admire. You'll also learn through the friends, colleagues, and mentors in your network. The goal is to ensure that we learn from history, live in the moment, and are prepared for the future.

Intelligence gathering focuses on these four subjects:

1   **GLOBAL TRENDS**—Events outside of everyone's collective control, such as financial markets, weather, politics, scientific discoveries, and cultural shifts. They are global situations

that could trickle down and impact your company, industry, and business in general.

2 **INDUSTRY DRIVING FORCES**—These factors influence your industry. This includes hiring practices, technology adoption, synthesis of roles, trends in mergers and acquisitions, insights into startups, and government regulations.

3 **360-DEGREE PERSPECTIVE OF COMPANIES**—This includes the public face (brand) and internal experience (culture) of the company. In what stage of evolution is your company? Is it a startup? Mature? In its best years? Its worst years? Is it expanding or contracting? What is its reputation in the industry?

4 **OPTIMIZING JOB PERFORMANCE**—This is the information and experiences that you gather to improve your skills, knowledge, and execution.

64

What are the sources of intelligence gathering?

During your intelligence gathering "expeditions," you'll find information from different sources, depending on the type of information you need. Following are five primary sources of information:

1 **SCHOLARLY RESEARCH**—Information you seek (primarily online or through a library) that is based on reports or studies, as opposed to news or opinion. Conducted by educational institutions, professional organizations, industry organizations, companies, or specific research groups about industries and businesses. (Applies to all four intelligence gathering subjects.)

2 **NEWS & INFORMATION**—Distributed through social media (LinkedIn, Facebook, Twitter, etc.), websites, blogs, apps, podcasts, TV, radio, newspaper, magazines, books, and documentaries. (Applies to all four subjects.)

3 **DEGREE PROGRAMS**—Degree programs, certifications, classes, seminars, workshops, or other sessions that are led by a professor or expert in a field or topic. (Applies to Optimizing Job Performance.)

4 **INFORMAL EDUCATION**—Focus on acquiring or improving skills that are job-specific or improve efficiency and success in general. Could also include software or hardware solutions and seminars, conferences, and webinars focused on niche audiences. (Applies to Optimizing Job Performance.)

5 **INSIDER INTELLIGENCE**— "Unofficial" information you receive from conversations with people inside or outside of your network, such as the job opportunities at a company, information

about a company's culture, or the behaviors of a potential co-worker or supervisor. (Primarily applies to Optimizing Job Performance and 360-Degree Perspective of Companies.)

65

What are sample statistics from scholarly research sources?

Use scholarly research to guide you in your career goals. When research-ing information, start with a list of questions you'd like to answer. For example, take a look at the first statistic. If you are searching for a VP role, it would be valuable to know how long it takes on average to find a VP job. Or, a little further down in the list, note that freelance jobs are on the rise, which may influence your decision to freelance rather than find a full-time job.

Following is a random sampling of statistics culled from schol-arly research.

- Average number of days to get hired = 43 (up to 76 days for VP or director roles)[115]
- Average percentage of man's pay a woman receives = 80%[116]
- Job that is held by the largest majority by men = Mason[117] Job that is held by the largest majority by women = Administrative Assistant[118]
- Percentage of full time jobs of total employment = 82%[119]
- Percent of the US workforce that will work freelancer either part- or full-time by 2020 = 50%[120]
- Average annual salary in cities in US in 2015 = $66,987[121]
- Average annual salary outside of major cities in US in 2015 = $52,081[122]
- Top 10 highest paying jobs (starting from highest):
  1 Surgeons/Anesthesiologists
  2 Orthodontists
  3 Physicians (various kinds)
  4 Chief Executives

5 Dentists

> **6** Nurse Anesthetists
>
> **7** Petroleum Engineers
>
> **8** Prosthodontists
>
> **9** Architectural & Engineering Managers
>
> **10** Podiatrists[123]

- Top 10 lowest paying jobs (starting from lowest):
  1 Fast Food Cook
  2 Food Prep/Server Combination
  3 Shampooer
  4 Dishwasher
  5 Seating Host/Hostess
  6 Counter Attendant/Barista
  7 Cashier
  8 Usher/Ticket Taker
  9 Amusement/Recreation Attendant
  10 Dining Room/Cafeteria Helper[124]

- Top 10 highest growth jobs (starting with highest):
  1 Wind Turbine Service Technician
  2 Occupational Therapist Assistant
  3 Physical Therapist Assistant
  4 Physical Therapist Aide
  5 Home Health Aide
  6 Commercial Diver
  7 Nurse Practitioner
  8 Physical Therapist
  9 Statistician
  10 Ambulance Driver/Attendant (not EMT)[125]

- Average cost of 4-year public college education in 2015 = $112,000[126]

- Average cost of 4-year private college education in 2015 = $236,000[127]

- Top 5 majors with best education cost vs annual salary ratio (starting with the highest return):
  1 Math (Research Analysis Manager)
  2 Information Technology (Business Intelligence Specialist, IT Mgr.)
  3 Human Resources (Compensation & Benefits Manager)
  4 Economics (Investment Operations Manager)
  5 Marketing (Product/Brand Manager)[128]
  6 Top 5 majors with worst education cost vs annual salary ratio (starting with the lowest return):
  7 Sociology (Social Worker, Corrections Officer)
  8 Fine Arts (Graphic Designer, Painter)
  9 Education (Teacher)
  10 Religious Studies/Theology (Pastor, Chaplain)
  11 Hospitality/Tourism (Event Planner, Hotel Manager)[129]
- Major US city with lowest unemployment = Boston, MA (2.5%, 2016)[130]
- Major US city with highest unemployment = Chicago, IL (5.4%, 2016)[131]
- Major US city with largest number of jobs = Orlando, FL (2017)[132]
- Major US city with lowest number of jobs = Detroit, MI (2017)[133]
- US city with largest growth of jobs = San Jose, CA[134]
- US industry with biggest growth = Home Healthcare Services (4.8% compound annual increase 2014-24)[135]
- US industry with biggest decline = Apparel, Leather and Allied Manufacturing (5.9% compound annual decrease 2014-24)[136]

66
What are sources for global trends?

For global trends, follow trusted news sources on a regular basis, and only do more in-depth, library-based research when planning a job or career change. Be aware of the economy, politics, government regulations and policies, and cultural changes that might affect your business. Don't forget to pay attention to what's happening in your industry outside of the U. S.

Here are a few trustworthy sources for tracking global trends with the descriptions from their websites:

- **PEW RESEARCH CENTER**—A nonpartisan fact tank that informs the public about the issues, attitudes and trends shaping America and the world. (https://www.pewresearch.org)
- **LIBRARY OF CONGRESS**—The Library of Congress is the largest library in the world and the main research arm of the U.S. Congress. (https://www.loc.gov)
- **THE WORLD FACTBOOK**—The World Factbook provides information on the history, people, government, economy, geography, communications, transportation, military, and transnational issues for 267 world entities. (https://www.cia.gov/library/publications/the-world-factbook/)
- **THE NATIONAL INTELLIGENCE COUNCIL (NIC)**—This agency serves as the US Intelligence Community's center for the long-term strategic analysis. The NIC's National Intelligence Officers, drawn from government, academia, and the private sector, are the IC's senior substantive experts on a range of issues. (https://www.dni.gov/index.php/global-trends-home)

67

How do I conduct industry-specific research?

Throughout your career journey, keep tabs on the innovations and best practices in your industry. Four activities that will keep you current are:

- Subscribe to industry blogs, newsletters, and publications
- Follow industry leaders on LinkedIn and Twitter
- Attend industry conferences and webinars
- Participate in industry organizations

68
How are companies structured?

Before you start you research on companies, be aware that there are essentially four different types of companies. You may naturally gravitate to one, but that can also change depending on your needs. For example, when you are starting out, you may want to work for a large corporation to gain a better understand of business operations in broad strokes and to meet numerous people to build your network. Later, you may decide a smaller business is more fitting.

National/multinational corporation
National, or multinational, companies are corporations that are publicly or privately held, have multiple locations, and are well-known brands. The Fortune 500 list is a good baseline list. It includes product and service companies in all industries: Google, Coke, General Motors, and Nike.

This company type is characterized by:

- High structure and stability, although some corporations annually "purge" the workforce of lowest performers to introduce "new blood" into the organization.
- Jobs are usually narrowly focused. In a small company, there might be a marketing professional who manages the social media channels, handles online advertising, and coordinates trade show materials. In a large corporation, there would be a manager exclusively for the company's Facebook channel.
- Difficulty moving quickly to respond to market trends or to be innovative.

Small Business

The Small Business Administration (SBA) defines a small business by size and gross revenue, but the exact requirements vary by industry. For manufacturing, small is defined as under 500 employees. For non-manufacturing, it is under $7.5 million in average annual receipts. Definitions vary more when using gross revenue. If a business is defined as "small," it does not mean that it only has one location, and it doesn't mean it was recently established. A small business could be a local store, an artisan, a designer, or a band. In fact, most businesses, 99.7%, in the U.S are small businesses.[137]

Startup

A startup is an early stage, innovative company, typically in the tech or medical fields. It is funded by investors who take a risk on the company because of the potential to grow fast, reach a large audience, and deliver large profits. Amazon is an example of a startup that evolved into a publicly-traded company.

Working at a startup means you might not do the same thing every day and will probably take on multiple roles. Usually fast-paced and sometimes chaotic, they are not a good place for someone who highly values security, but taking a risk on a startup could mean a big reward. Typically, the salary is less, but employees earn a small partial ownership in the company.

Nonprofit

Just because a company is called a "nonprofit" doesn't mean that it doesn't make money. It means the revenue earned does not benefit any individual; it is cycled back into the organization. The nonprofit income is tax exempt through the 501(3)(C) status because it is providing a benefit to a community.

Generally, nonprofits are smaller and operate at a slower pace, although there are many large, well-established nonprofits like the Red Cross and ASPCA. Because nonprofits are not trying to make more and more money, they tend to have a more "family" feel, with people who are passionate about their work. Usually, the same job title will be paid less than at a startup or corporation, and you may not be working with the latest MacBook or most current software. The work environment is not cutting edge or outfitted with many, or any, perks.

69

How can I find out about potential occupations?

When I started college, I didn't know what roles I could get with my Bachelor of Fine Arts (BFA) degree. Today, you can scour online job boards, a company's career website, or information supplied by the government to examine how industries are structured and what jobs are available in each industry.

One government-generated resource, The Occupational Outlook Handbook (OOH) at BLS.gov, can help you to:

- Understand how industries and the jobs within them are categorized
- Learn about job titles that you didn't know existed
- Investigate the various industries to which your skills could apply
- Learn the status of an industry (e.g. is it on the upswing or in a downturn?)

The OOH lists 328 jobs in 25 categories. Review it to understand how jobs in the U.S. are organized. Let's analyze the breakdown of jobs in the States. Per the Bureau of Labor Statistics, "[i]n July 2017, the majority of the U.S. workforce, 102.6 million people (71% of all nonfarm payroll employees) worked in private service-providing industries."[138] The report broke that total down into the following major sectors:

- Education and Health Services (22.7 million)
- Government (22.2 million, two-thirds at the local level)
- Professional and Business Services (20.3 million)
- Retail Trade (16 million)
- Manufacturing (12.3 million)[139]

In addition, each state's Department of Labor provides information about several parameters of occupations and the job market. Some statistics you can expect to find through your state's Department of Labor website are:

- Number of jobs per sector
- Labor market highlights by month
- Unemployment rates

"The North American Industry Classification System (NAICS) is the standard used by Federal statistical agencies to classify business establishments for the purpose of collecting, analyzing, and publishing statistical data related to the U.S. business economy."[140]

You can utilize NAICS to:

- Understand how an industry's job are categorized
- Learn about job titles that you didn't know existed
- Investigate the various industries in which your skills could apply

70

How do I conduct company-specific research?

If you are interested in working for a company, start by visiting their website. Go through the website with a fine-tooth comb and learn everything you can about the company. Be sure to read their annual report which is usually posted.

Culture

It is unlikely that you will find this spelled out, but you can read between the lines by assessing the brand feel: formal, playful, innovative, etc. Although assessing a company's culture is best accomplished by working there, the next best thing is to speak with current or former employees.

Be aware that culture can vary greatly between departments. The culture of a company or department greatly influences how you feel when working there. It can be strict or relaxed regarding working from home, the number of hours worked, dress code, and how teams interact, to name just a few areas to consider.

Values

Most companies define their values on their website. Compare them against your own. Again, do your best to read between the lines. For example, if a company says that they support their employees, that can be executed in many ways. Support can mean empowering them to make decisions, being nurturing. It can also mean that employees have very few decisions to make because senior management makes all the decisions—in other words, because the company is authoritarian. Aligning with a company's values is the most important part of your assessment of them.

Careers

This section of the website offers information for those looking to become employees of the company and can be segmented into several components. A job bank lists currently available jobs, typically divided into recent grads and professionals. Sometimes, postings may not be current, and remember that not all roles are publicly posted. Information about the hiring process can be listed, even sharing specific interview questions and other requirements to help you succeed in an interview. There may be employee profiles, and sometimes video interviews. This will help you assess employee diversity, culture, dress, and attitudes.

Board of directors/advisors

Review the site to evaluate the allegiances the company has with other companies, to gain a sense of their politics, and to look for diversity. Note the language used by executives in their bios and how they speak about the company.

Corporate responsibility

A company's behaviors and relationships express the company's values. If a company claims to value being "green," but then partners with a known environmental offender, that demonstrates a conflict.

Companies reveal themselves on their websites and in other media outlets, in ways that align with their brands. They are hoping to attract people that will "fit" in their company. Hiring the wrong person is a costly venture. Companies spend approximately $8,000 for training, advertising, management, and HR time to replace a single wrong hire.[141] Companies spend an average of $2,936 on HR per employee per year.[142]

Still, the company website is giving you their biased assessment of themselves. That is why it's important to get a more unbiased view of a company through other methods.

A great resource is the website glassdoor.com, a site where current and previous employees rate and review their experiences. Each company is evaluated through "company reviews, CEO approval ratings, salary reports, interview reviews and questions, [and] benefits reviews."[143] You are hearing directly from the people who have experienced the culture. It's not perfect. You may get a disgruntled employee with a skewed perspective, but comparable to a site like Yelp!, you can get an impression from crowdsourcing.

Another option is to speak directly to a current or previous employee of the company. "Insider intelligence," as I call it, can give you access to info related to upcoming job opportunities, the behavior of employees, the company culture, and other aspects of the company only known by "insiders." This information is gained directly from employees or others who work directly with the company. Of course, this explicitly does not refer to trade secrets or other company info that legally cannot be shared. Even a short conversation could provide insightful, nuanced information.

To find an "insider," start by checking your LinkedIn network and search for the company of interest. Reach out to contacts with a first degree of connection first. If you don't have direct contacts in the company, ask for a referral from a contact who does have a connection at the company. If you strike out on LinkedIn, try friends and family, or possibly reach out through your university or alumni career services department or instructors.

Lastly, you can research companies through various websites, publications, and databases. You can learn about their histories, relationships with other companies, legal problems, financial statuses, prominent employees, successful ventures and various other useful tidbits.

If it's a public company, you can find a wealth of information through Hoovers.com, MarketWatch, SEC.gov, or other financial websites. Through databases such as Hoovers, you can download lists of companies based on your industry of interest. For example, if you'd like to illustrate comic books, you can check for publishers. Start by creating a list of smaller publishers. Select two to three companies to contact for an informational interview.

To access these databases, go to the Science, Industry, and Business library (SIB) on 34th Street in New York City, or find a comparable library resource in your college or town. Since companies pay thousands of dollars a year for access to some of these databases, take advantage of any that you can access for free with your library card. The SIB library provides free classes on job searching skills including how to research.

Researching non-publicly traded (private) companies can be more problematic. The best source is a database accessible from libraries called Reference USA. Otherwise, check trade publications and online sources for industry news that mentions the company of interest.

71

How do I assess if I'm a "good fit" with a company?

Deciding on what company you'd like to work for is a big decision. How do you know if you'd like working there? Start with a list of the top ten companies you admire and for which you'd like to work. Then use the checklist below to assess your compatibility:

1. **SITUATIONAL PREFERENCES**—Do you like the location, hours, work environment, perks, and other tangible parameters?

2. **SHARED VALUES**—Do you see the world the same way? Do you agree with the values stated by the company? Although a company may declare their values one way, they might be expressed differently in the work environment. Try to read between the lines. Check with current employees to determine how the company's values are expressed in the workplace.

3. **CULTURAL FIT**—Every company has their own company culture. The culture is created, in most cases, in an unconscious way and derived from the company's vision and values and the behaviors and interactions of the employees. The culture manifests in an "ambiance" in the office. Google's culture presents as a sense of excitement, innovation, competition, and intelligence. American Express is homogenous, smart, and hierarchical. Would you thrive or starve in either one? Many companies have cited a fit with company culture as more important than skills because a good fit must occur naturally.

4 **CURRENTLY A CUSTOMER** (if relevant)—If the company produces a consumer-facing product or service, are you one of their customers? Ideally, you would be. If you're not a customer, would you feel good about working there?

5 **POTENTIAL FOR GROWTH**—Could you imagine yourself working and growing at the company over the span of your career? Some of the best leaders started from the bottom ranks and moved up, learning every aspect of the business. Ursula Burns started as an intern at Xerox. After twenty-nine years with the company, she earned the title of CEO. It doesn't mean you have to stay at the company for a lifetime; just gauge the longer-term opportunities.

After you evaluate each parameter above, there is no better barometer than working there. Consider an internship, a freelance project, or a contract position before accepting a full-time position.

If your company research leads you to the conclusion that a company would be a good fit, the next step is to evolve a relationship with the company.

1 Add them to your "My companies to work for" list
2 Gather news about them automatically through a news reader
3 Connect to the company's and top executive's social media channels
4 Search your network for employees to get "insider intelligence"
5 Set up job searches through online job boards and the company's website

72
Why should I volunteer?

If you're not in school, can't land an internship, or want to try a new field, volunteering is a great option to test a role, get experience, and network. When volunteering, you can try out newly-learned skills in a real-life environment. For example, if you just conducted your first competitive research project while on the job, you could offer that service to a nonprofit and increase your experience. You can also volunteer a service that you have developed outside of work, such as writing Facebook copy. If you deliver your service as a volunteer, add it to your resume.

How do you find a volunteer position? There are websites, like <u>Volunteer Match</u>, that connect volunteers with nonprofits that need help. Alternatively, you may know of a nonprofit that supports a cause you're passionate about. Contact them to see if they need what you're offering. Most nonprofits can use marketing support materials: websites, social media support, outreach materials, videos, etc.

If you are working for a small nonprofit, it may not have a formal volunteer program. If that's the case, offer to volunteer for a specific amount of time to deliver a project. Defining the expectations will make success easier to achieve. Be sure you report to just one person.

When you are ready to volunteer, connect with an organization that aligns with your values and offers an opportunity to hone your existing skills in a new context or gain more experience in a new skill. In return for donating your services, you gain valuable experience applicable to your next fee-based opportunity. Include your volunteer work in your resume or portfolio.

Through volunteering, you'll connect with new people and may get inside information about your industry. For example, if you are a designer and volunteer for the Freelancers Union, you might learn about proposed legislation before others in your field.

73

What is the value of an internship, and how do I find one?

Today, you absolutely need an internship while you're in school. When I was in college, internships weren't as prevalent. Instead, I created my own internships by working part-time since high school. I painted murals for bar mitzvahs, designed floral arrangements, counted inventory in supermarkets and painted houses. In each job, I learned how to improve my skills, lead and take directions, and communicate in the professional world.

There are three reasons why you need an internship. First, because an internship will help you decide if you like a job. It may look good on paper, but you won't know if you like it until you do it every day. Second, when you graduate you'll need to show professional experience on your resume and, if relevant, a portfolio demonstrating professional experience. You can list your internship. Lastly, in an internship you can learn about how your field works and start to sense your strengths and weaknesses. When you have real-life professional constraints, you will grow faster—someone directing you, limited time to complete work, client requirements, and general work stress factors.

Nancy is a Dean at a major university. Following is her perspective on internships:

> Internships (paid or unpaid) are one of the best methods to "test the waters" of a given career path. Most schools will have established internship programs that students can access or a student can bring an opportunity to the student services personnel at their school and request to have it set up as an internship. Not only does the internship appear on the official transcript but students can build their resumes as well as

request references and/or letters of recommendation from the host businesses.

A less formal method, but one I have personally experienced is looking for ways to get out of your comfort zone. Take on challenging projects. Do things you have never tried. Volunteer. Study abroad. Take risks. I've always felt that nothing worthwhile is easy. Don't be afraid to fail.[144]

74

What formal education and/ or training do I need?

If you know what job or career you'd like to pursue, research the educational requirements. Check out the site bls.gov for information about jobs and their educational requirements, in which states they are located, salary ranges, and market trends. With the high cost of some formal education programs today, it is essential to understand the reality of the job market, and the requirements of your job of choice, before investing in education.

If you are not sure what job or career is of interest, then consider taking courses that pique your curiosity. Delve into each course before concluding that it's not worth further exploration. It takes time to assess a subject.

You can also decide to pursue a career without college. According to the report, 30% of the 47 million new jobs expected to be created in the U.S. by 2018 will only require an associate's degree or a certificate.[145]

Following is a breakdown of degrees that may be listed as educational requirements:

- Secondary School (high school or GED)
- Associates Degree (2 years of college)
- Bachelor's Degree (4 years of college)
- Master's Degree (2 years of postgraduate college)
- Doctoral or Professional Degree (4+ years of postgraduate college)
- Postsecondary Non-Degree

All degrees beyond secondary school have an area of focus. A BFA is a Bachelor of Fine Arts which covers visual arts. A MBA is a Master's of Business Administration covering marketing, finance, or business management.

There are also licenses required to work in various fields even beyond the Bachelor's, Master's, or Doctorate degrees. For example, to become a social worker, in addition to a Master's of Social Work, you will need a Licensed Clinical Social Worker (LCSW) license before being allowed to practice. Requirements for licenses can vary from state to state in the U.S.

College

Most people in the United States today still take the route of higher education to start their career; 69.2% of 2015 high school graduates enrolled in college immediately.[146] That wasn't always the case. Before World War I, less than 5% of the college-aged attended college.[147]

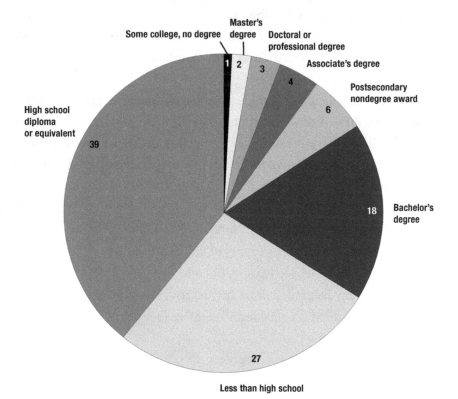

As you can see in the chart, 67% of the jobs in the US require a high school diploma or less. For the 18% of jobs that require a Bachelor's Degree, the average salary is $68,190. Curiously enough, the 2% of jobs that require a Master's Degree have a lower average salary of $64,510. Finally, 3% of jobs require a PHD, and the average salary for those jumps to $97,550.[148]

If we do a little math, we find that 23% of jobs require a Bachelor's Degree or higher. However, in 2015, 33% of US population had a Bachelor's Degree.[149] More people today are earning their college degrees than ever, but the educational requirements of jobs are not keeping up with our increasingly educated population.

Vocational training

This form of education is very functional. Its aim is to give you the exact skills you need to perform a specific trade upon graduation. The jobs that are served by vocational training, such as dental hygienists or electricians, typically do not include a path to a higher level. A 2011 study by the Harvard Graduate School of Education stated that "30% of the 47 million new jobs expected to be created in the U.S. by 2018 will only require an associate's degree or a certificate."[150]

Continuing education

Continuing education provides a wide variety of programs for students that have already completed undergraduate, graduate, or doctoral programs at a university. It can include skills training for specific jobs, workplace-based training, online courses, formal personal enrichment, and more. The program may or may not offer a certificate or other acknowledgement of completion.

Continuing education is offered through separate entities of colleges (like NYU's School of Professional Studies), organizations (such as the American Marketing Association's Professional Certified Marketer certification), and industry specific training. There are online continuing education platforms as well. Lynda.com is a well-established website that offers subscription-based access to a library of online videos for creative industries, marketing, and digital fields. Coursera.org offers online courses (and some certificates) for classes from well-known institutions such as Princeton and Stanford.

Learning approach

The methods of teaching listed above do not work for everyone. For instance, dyslexics may struggle with the reading requirements of online classes. "There is a higher incidence of dyslexia in entrepreneurs in the USA than in the normal and corporate populations. Thirty-five percent of US entrepreneurs…reported as dyslexic but less than 1% of corporate managers, this compares with a US national incidence of up 15%."[151] Becoming an entrepreneur without a college education may not be the typical career path, but it is most certainly just as valid as any other.

Everyone learns in different ways. Some learn by reading and writing notes. Other learn best by listening to a professor speak and digesting that info. A good percentage learn best by trial and error. It's very important to know which method works best for you.

75

How do I find the salary range for a profession?

Researching everything about the job you are considering makes you a "smart shopper." Choosing a job solely for its financial benefits may not be the most satisfactory path for most people, but you should know the salary range for jobs that you're considering. Be realistic about your salary/benefits wants and needs.

It's easy to find out what jobs are the highest paying. Following are three options. First, the U.S. government documents salary information through the Bureau of Labor Statistics, bls.gov. Data is organized by several parameters—state, metropolitan region, industry, occupation, and job characteristics—so you can search for what you need

Second, Glassdoor.com documents salary ranges by title and company, based on information volunteered by contributors who work in the industry. Enter a job title and location, and find the local and national salaries for that positions.

Lastly, you can access salary information on payscale.com. First, respond to a series of survey questions. Then, after submitting your email, results are displayed on screen and you receive a report with salary estimates for the job you selected.

In 2016, the jobs with the highest pay were concentrated in the medical professions, business, and technology. The top job, clocked at $246,320 per year, was an anesthesiologist. Of the top twenty, fourteen were medical, ranging from Pharmacist to Podiatrist.[152]

The Job Search Life Cycle

All of what we've discussed to this point is prep work for the actual job search. By now, you've made progress on self-awareness, understand how to grow your network and relationships, have researched your industry and potential employers, and have an idea of what type of role is right for you in today's economic, social, and political climate.

Although we have discussed the various employment types, from this point on, we will focus on the life cycle of searching for a full-time job, with a focus on corporation positions. It's a cycle because you will likely go through this process more than ten times in your career, and that's if you have consecutive full-time jobs. The market is moving away from full-time employees; "nearly 35% of today's total workforce is comprised of non-employee worker, including temps, freelancers, statement of work (SOW) based labor, independent contractors, etc."[153] Knowing the process puts you in control.

76

What is the full-time job search life cycle?

Key components of the job search in the full-time job life cycle include finding job openings, filling out applications, interviewing, and negotiating a contract.

What are the key phases of a job?

Every job has a life cycle that includes how you:

- Search for the job and win the job
- Succeed in the job
- Transition to the next job

You may love the actual job, but not the finding it or terminating it. For example, I co-produced and hosted a local cable TV show. A network executive saw me on the show and invited me to her office. She said, "Hey, we'd love you host this new TV show." I thought, "That sounds like a great job!" Then, I went on the audition, and it was a total disaster because I had zero experience or knowledge about the audition process!

But, but got me interested in becoming a TV host. I took a couple of acting classes and went on a few auditions. I quickly realized that as much as I would love hosting a show, I hated the audition process more that I wanted to host a show!

For many careers, there is a progression from a task-based specialist to executive leadership. For example, my path started as a designer. As a designer, I was responsible for doing the work assigned to me. The first level of management responsibilities was hiring people that supported my tasks, such as writers, illustrators, and typographers. Next, I started directing a team of creatives which included all of the above. Shortly afterwards, I was managing the systems, technologies, and processes that supported the team. Ultimately, I had to learn how the creative team fit into the larger picture of the success of the business.

This doesn't mean that you must follow a path up through management to be successful. Alternatively, I could have strived to become the best designer. Consider what will sustain your interest and how you will define success. Know the entire life cycle of the job, then decide if you can tolerate the worst parts of the life cycle in exchange for the best!

77

How do I plan for a job search?

Create an action plan

Getting a great job takes planning, focus, and follow-through. Start off with a written plan that includes the actions below. Treat your job search like a project and follow good project management procedures for success: define your goals, create a timeline, and schedule milestones which could include the subtitles on this page.

Decide on the job title

Based on the results of your self-awareness evaluations and your intelligence gathering, analyze job descriptions and decide on a job title to use in your search. To define the job, think about what you will be doing in the role and note the various job titles, keywords, and phrases associated with the role. If you are looking to lead a team of developers and designers to create apps, you could search for "digital director," "creative," and "VP creative."

To get a good pulse on what jobs are available, use job metasearch sites like Indeed or SimplyHired. Use keywords that describe the job or part of the job title to get a feel for the volume of jobs, what companies are hiring, and if you have any gaps in the skills typically required.

Make a "top ten" list of companies

After you decide on a job title and review the marketplace, make a list of ten companies you'd love to work for. The idea of creating a top ten list was given to me by a family friend. He insisted that I look at only the top ad agencies when I started my job search. Set your expectations high. It's easier to lower them if you are not getting traction.

To create the list, pull from companies that you have researched and found to be a match: companies you respect or companies from which you purchase products and services. Consider what companies are admired in your field of interest. What companies are innovative and have a bright future? Who has a reputation for treating their employees well? Many publications issue "best places to work" compilations annually. Make sure you write the final list, and not just have it in your head.

Keep in mind that having a top-rated, recognized brand on your resume acts like a gold star. It validates you, and you receive a halo effect from their positive brand.

Check for contacts at those companies

Cindy is a top HR executive and suggests:

> The best way to increase your chances of being contacted in response to a job posting is to get introduced as an employee referral. Do your homework and try to find a connection through networking or through LinkedIn.
>
> Many companies have formal employee referral programs that have financial incentives for employees when a referral gets hired.
>
> Employee referrals are always considered before other candidates are reviewed.[154]

Arrange an informational interview with your contact. If you don't have a direct contact, check if any of your primary contacts can refer you to someone. Also, research where you could meet people from the company. Do they attend or speak at conferences? Support any causes? Participate in job fairs?

Your contacts provide support in two ways. First, they can be your reference for posted jobs. Second, they can inform you of any upcoming jobs that are not publicly posted. The earlier you're informed about a job, the more likely you are to be able to minimize the competitive pool. If a few employees give referrals to the hiring manager, they might just interview that handful of people without broadening the search.

Document your progress

As you work through your Action Plan, track your contacts, company list, applications, job descriptions, interviewer's names, contact info, and dates of interviews or related communications. Focus on your top ten list but also follow up on other opportunities as they present themselves.

Working in parallel

If you are looking for a job and not currently employed, consider contract or freelance work. In addition to providing an income, it keeps you engaged and in touch with other opportunities. Although it takes time and energy to find new full-time employment, it's best to keep working while looking. A working person is perceived better by a potential employer. They like the idea of "stealing" the best from a competitor, as opposed to hiring someone that isn't employed.

If it's not possible to work while job searching, ensure your savings account will cover two to three months of expenses, a little more than the average time it takes to find a full-time job.[155] If you are in school, check with career services. If you are an alumnus, most universities provide career support services.

78
How do I analyze a job description?

A job is a conglomerate of activities, contributions, situations, decisions, relationships, and perceptions that form the "anatomy" of that job. Together, these components form the experience you will have working at that job.

Job descriptions focus on the activities, and very superficially, the relationships, involved in a job. It typically defines the job title, major tasks, reporting structure (relationships), required skills and education, and location, but it is very difficult to discern what situations and decision-making you'll experience and the complexities and politics of the relationships from a job description.

To better make the decision about if a job is right for you, you'll have to research beyond the job description.

Start by analyzing a job description using this five step-technique.

1 Definitions
2 Read through it on a literal level to assure you understand the requirements. If there is something you don't understand, for example a software, an acronym, a technique or system, research it.
3 Interpretation
4 Now, read again and read between the lines. Although job descriptions are written in a formal way, you can sometimes get a sense of the job from how responsibilities (or other parts of the description) are written.
5 Mapping
6 Map your resume to the job, literally. Do your experience and skills cover at least 75% of what is being requested?[156]

7 Context

8 Compare the description to the same or similar job titles at other companies. How do they differ? Within the company, does it look like there are several openings? Are there several openings with the same job title? Does it seem that the company is going through a hiring spree, or is it shrinking? Does the company have high turnover (you can track that over several visits)?

9 Job titles vary from company to company. For example, job duties defined in one financial services company as a Director role, are classified as a Vice President role at another company. The size and the culture of the company influences how job descriptions are written and the depth and breadth of responsibilities that fall under a specific title.

10 Creative Visualization

11 Imagine yourself doing the job. Try using the technique of creative visualization. Close your eyes, and start from waking up in the morning. What time is it? What are you going to wear? Do you have time for breakfast? How do you travel to the office? How is the office decorated? Who do you work with (based what you've gleaned from the job description)? What is your supervisor like? What work are you doing? Continue imagining right up to when you leave the office.

Following is an actual job posting from Google. In italics, I show what questions you could ask when reviewing the highlighted area of the job description.

Product Strategy and Operations Lead (Example)

The Business Strategy & Operations organization provides business-critical insights, ensures cross-functional alignment of goals and goal executions, and helps teams drive strategic partnerships and new initiatives forward. We stay focused on aligning the highest-level company priorities with strong day-to-day operations, and help evolve early stage ideas into future-growth initiatives.

This is a top-level digital management job with the responsibility of delivering on key company goals while managing a likely busy and diverse global team and running research and development for new revenue generating products.

Our ecosystem is constantly growing and evolving, and it is critical to deploy resources efficiently to best serve our users, creators and advertisers globally.

This job is fast-paced and goals could be a moving target. Since it is a global company, there may be late hours to communicate with other time zones.

We believe in using data to drive the decisions we make every day. You will be responsible for driving how we use data at our company as well as providing insights into our business and strategic direction based on data analysis.

Data is mentioned in many forms throughout this job descriptions and is the primary keyword. Knowing how to create systems to capture data, analyze data, and use data to create visualization to communicate to others is important.

As a Product Strategy & Operations Lead, you will be a close business partner to our teams of Data Scientists, combining your business insight and judgment with their deep analytical horsepower.

You will be the business lead but will need to know how to communicate with data scientists, which could be challenging.

> You will ensure that we have the right tools, data visualization and processes to deliver analytical insights to the organization that drive product decisions.

> You will be aligned against specific company products and work cross-functionally with many of the company's teams that manage each of these products: Product, Engineering, UX, Finance, Marketing, HR and Sales. You will become an expert on the company's data and a consultant on how to use data to operate our business and make important strategic decisions.

You are a business person, but will need to understand each of these teams to know how data can help them make decisions. That means you also need to be an excellent communicator. This is a unique skill set: business, data science, communications and digital products.

> Our company has grown into a community used by over XX number of people across the globe to access information, share content, and shape culture. The company team helps budding creators build careers, create products, and engages communities around shared passions and global conversations. Together, we empower the world to create, and share.

Responsibilities

> Collaborate with our product and strategy teams to understand how our own performance relates to the broader industry.

Source and analyze market insights.

> Drive the design for our internal data tools that are used to communicate data throughout company and the parent company, and work closely with Product Managers and Engineers as they develop these tools.

Lead the design and development of custom built products for data management.

> Deliver metric reporting for leadership across our company and parent company—senior leaders, our Board of Directors, Sales teams and others.

This role requires communication directly with senior leadership, therefore, you should be comfortable with public speaking and presentations. The sales team is important as they are mentioned specifically.

> Partner with our Data Science team to prioritize and execute sophisticated quantitative analyses and advanced modeling that deliver actionable insights to our product and engineering teams.

> Prepare presentations and clearly communicate findings from initiatives to senior management and to the broader organization.

Qualifications

Minimum qualifications:
You will need this to get into the door, but it is unlikely you'll get the job unless you have 2-3 of the preferred qualifications.

- BA/BS degree in technical or business field or equivalent practical experience.

- 6 years of experience in an analytical role, such as management consulting, investment banking, business intelligence, data science or corporate strategy.
- Experience with data analysis, modeling and SQL.

This term may require some research if you don't know what it means.

- Experience presenting data and findings to stakeholders.

Preferred Qualifications

- MBA or advanced degree.
- Experience in consumer internet, media or online media industries.
- Experience building software products, either as a product manager or engineer.
- Experience in data/statistical analysis workflow (e.g. R, Python, STATA, MATLAB).

These terms may require research if you don't know what they mean.

- Experience in computer science, statistics, machine learning, or financial analysis.[157]

79

Where can I find job openings?

There are several ways to find job openings. Following are some suggestions listed in order of importance. While you are waiting for a response from one task, you can begin the next.

Connect with your prospective employers

Visit the websites of your top 10 companies, and create a profile in their career sections. In the profile, you can save one or more resumes and cover letters for each application. It will also remember your contact info so that you don't have to enter it for each application. If a company on your list doesn't have a career section, check for a Facebook or LinkedIn presence. If you can't find that either, email or call the main contact to ask the best way to stay in touch about job openings.

Sign up for job lists from various organizations

Certain organizations—such as government agencies, professional associations, and publications/blogs—compile lists of jobs that might interest their members or community. Many offer alerts based on parameters that you customize. Consider creating an email filter that directs all these emails into one folder in your email client. That way, you can allot a certain amount of time each day to check for new alerts.

Contact your college or its alumni network

If you are in college, contact your career counselor. Most universities provide job placement services that will help you get started, but don't fully rely on them to get a job for you! Ask to see their placement statistics, and find out how most students in your school land jobs. Many times, universities have relationships with certain corporations that offer preferential hiring.

If you are out of school, get in touch with your alumni network. Many have websites and a social media presence as well. Attend events if you live in proximity to the school. If not, contact alumni through the channels provided. Many alumni networks post job openings and host job fairs.

Search job aggregator websites

Job aggregator websites—like Indeed, LinkUp, and SimplyHired—pull listings from their original sources to present them through one platform. However, only 37% of jobs are filled through online job boards.[158] As long as job aggregators are not the only method you are using to find a job, continue filling out applications!

In addition, use these sites to assess what is happening in the job marketplace in real time. What companies are hiring for your role? Has the industry shifted to a new location? Are many companies hiring for your role? This could mean your position is in high demand and you could be in a better position for negotiating. Sign up for several alerts based on varying parameters: job title (with minimal keywords), location, industry, etc.

Communicate to your network through LinkedIn or other channels

Let your network know you are looking for an opportunity. Use LinkedIn to post articles to show your expertise. This will be posted on the daily feed so others will see your name. It might make them more likely to think of you if they hear of a relevant job opening.

Attend a job fair or networking event

A job fair is an event where businesses present their company's immediate and potential opportunities. Bring your business card and resume, and have a pitch ready. You may also be asked to fill out forms. Many times, job fairs are organized to present internship opportunities.

Networking events are sometimes designed for job opportunities as well. As an example, a school that trains developers may invite web design companies and startups to meet the latest graduating class.

Work with recruiters

Check the next FAQ for detailed info on working with recruiters.

Kelin is a recruiter with a large global recruiting firm. Following is her advice on how to find your next job:

> The tried and true methods in many ways have not changed. The BEST way is and has always been to network and find connections that will help you with your next job opportunity. When looking for a job always start with your connections: friends, former colleagues, family, and anybody they might know. LinkedIn is the latest tool to help with this process and a great place to start. Make sure your LinkedIn Profile is up to date with your latest resume, skills, and whenever possible get endorsements from your network.
>
> Scour the LinkedIn site and make connections with anyone and everyone you ever worked with that you would be able to reach out to for information on a job posting. Many recruiters use LinkedIn as their go-to tool for finding qualified candidates so the more content and connections you have the more likely they are to find you. If they know someone in your network, then they are even more likely to reach out to you.
>
> Secondly, don't give up on the basics of job searching. Do your homework; research companies in your market that are of interest to you and go to their websites to review their career postings. Using an online tool like indeed.com will expedite this process, too. With Indeed you can set up search parameters to be able to get notifications sent to you when companies post jobs that match your skills. It's a great tool that aggregates companies' job postings.
>
> Thirdly, reach out to recruiters and let them work on your behalf to find that next great job! If you have a skill set that is highly technical or niche, you can research recruiting firms that source for those skills. For instance, there are many

recruiting firms that source for creative jobs like design, marketing, writing etc. In addition, there are a multitude of technical recruiting firms for jobs in the engineering & IT industries. There are even recruiting firms that focus on manufacturing and administrative services. The thing to remember is that they are bringing the career opportunity to you; they might already have a strong working relationship with the company, HR, and hiring managers so you are better off getting the job through them than on the open market.

Don't be afraid to take a role that starts out as a temporary position but might later have the potential to become a full-time role. Many companies prefer to hire this way and it's a win-win for everyone involved.[159]

80
Should I work with a recruiter?

The global staffing market, of which recruiters are a part, is huge: "in 2013 [it] was worth an estimated USD$416 billion (using sales rather than gross profit)."[160] Therefore, even though job sites have facilitated direct connections between employer and candidates, there is still a big place for intermediaries. The staffing market includes everything from freelancers to offshore hires.

The role of the recruiter is to facilitate the connection between the candidate and the employer. Typically, recruiters specialize in certain industries or skills and have relationships with employers, but not all recruiters are created equal. Some do not add much value and will only present with you with opportunities you could have easily found yourself.

The best way to find a recruiter is to ask colleagues with similar positions which recruiters they respect. If you are in school, it's possible your career counselor may have suggestions. Make sure the recruiter is an expert in your industry and that they work with the companies on your top ten list. Engage with recruiters who understand what is important to you. Build relationships with good recruiters, as they can support you throughout your career.

Sometimes recruiters may reach out to you through LinkedIn or via email. Background check them and their company before agreeing to a call. Do not sign any documents until you are sure you want to work with them.

81

What is job shadowing, and how do I arrange it?

Job shadowing is the act of following someone during their work activities to get a sense of their job. Think of it as an abbreviated version of an apprenticeship. Job shadowing can last from a half day up to a week. There is no payment to the shadower for their time.

To arrange for job shadowing, first ask colleagues in your network if they know of someone who is working in the role you want. Also, check with your career counselor. Certain nonprofit organizations offer job shadowing through corporations with whom they have partnerships.

While you are shadowing, you may be asked to execute certain tasks. This is at the discretion of the person who you are shadowing. During the experience, new aspects of the job may come to light. That is the point. You can only know a job by doing it. A job shadower once told me that he had no idea that my role as the lead of a creative department would be so meeting-centric!

82
What is an informational interview, and what can I ask?

In addition to job shadowing and reviewing the company's website and media coverage, the best way to get a sense of working for a company is through an informational interview. What is an informational interview? It is not an interview for a specific job, but a meeting with a company employee to understand what it's like to work there, to review the organizational chart (the list of jobs and the reporting structure) of departments you're interested in, and to build a relationship with an employee that may help you in your future endeavors to get employed.

> The concept of the informational interview (also known as an informational conversation) was first introduced by Richard N. Bolles, author of the popular job-search book, *What Color is Your Parachute?* Bolles believes that job seekers should speak with professionals in their field of interest to gather more information before choosing a particular career path.[161]

How do you schedule an informational interview? It will primarily be arranged through your network. Remember you're asking someone to give their precious time. Be respectful of that. What does the employee get out of it? They may be able to look good if they introduce a great new employee to the company. Many companies provide a referral fee for introducing a candidate that is hired. It's also a chance build a new relationship that may help them in the future as well.

Typically, an informational interview is a short phone conversation, but it could be in person depending on what your contact can set up. Remember to send a thank you letter, and ask if you can stay in touch on LinkedIn.

Informational interview questions

Below are nine questions you can ask during your next informational interview to make the most of this valuable opportunity.

1   What path did you take to arrive at this role?
2   What are your favorite and least favorite aspects of this role and why?
3   What skills and personality traits do you think are best for a person in this role?
4   What's a typical day like for you?
5   Does this role have direct reports?
6   What is a typical team size for this role?
7   What is the best way to evaluate if I would be good in this role?
8   What is the natural progression after this role?
9   What networking groups or professional associations do you suggest I join?

83

What does "building a campaign" mean?

Once you find a job to apply for, you'll need to establish support for your candidacy. Like a candidate running for political office, it's beneficial if you build a "campaign" to support your "election" to that job. Building a campaign entails contacting those you know who work at the company. Contact no more than three people, and let them know you are interested in the job. Share the job description and your resume, and ask if you'd be a good fit, whether they know the hiring manager or team, and if they could support your candidacy once you apply. Be sure to ask in a way that doesn't make them feel uncomfortable to say "no." There may be political reasons why they cannot support you. It doesn't necessarily mean they don't value you or your work.

Request that your contact tell the hiring manager that you'd be a great member of the team. Be sure to thank them, whether you land the job or not. It could be as simple as a written card.

If you don't know anyone at the company, try using LinkedIn to find first or second level contacts who could reach out to their networks to find people who can support your campaign.

Luke is an expert networker and a natural at making connections. He shares valuable advice regarding how to request support from your network:

The "ghosting" technique

(The below is especially applicable to job searching, but has many other applications.)

We all get help from others when networking, and one of the most effective ways to get people to introduce you is to save them time by ghosting the email. I also call it a "strawman" or "starter email." This basically means writing a text template that they can adjust and send out on your behalf.

It saves a huge amount of time for everyone, but most importantly, for the "helper" all while guiding him/her to say what you want.

Websites do this all the time for social sharing—they create the text for you to post to social networks. You're usually free to change it, but it increases the likelihood that you will post because they've started for you. I'm always shocked more people don't do this for professional intros; it's probably done only 5% of the time.

Job search example

Let's say Lisa has worked at a small ad agency for three years as an Account Executive, but she now wants a role at a larger agency. She has an informational interview with an Account Supervisor at a target firm. There aren't relevant openings there, but the "helper" (we'll call her Michelle) offers to make a couple intros to friends and former colleagues at a couple of other firms.

If Lisa says thank you and forwards a resume or LinkedIn profile, I give it about a 25% chance that Michelle will follow through, depending on any number of factors—how busy she is the next couple days, how polite/appreciative Lisa is, Lisa's follow-up, how "networky" Michelle is, etc. Lisa can easily double or quadruple Michelle's chances of following through by ghosting the note for her.

To that effect, her thank you note could be something like:

Hi Michelle,

I appreciate your time today, and enjoyed hearing about <ABC aspects of Michelle's firm/experience/advice>.

I hoped you could indeed introduce me to A, B, and C, who work at Agencies X, Y, and Z. I hope it's okay that I ghosted a note in the effort to save you time. Change it as you wish, or I can send another version to adjust the length/tone, etc.

Possible subject line: Intro request: Lisa, an AE curious about Agency X

Hi _____,

I met with Lisa today, who has three years' experience as an AE at a boutique ad agency called AgencyName, working on the AccountName, specifically on Product/ServiceName. She also worked for a year doing AnotherJobTitle.

Even if Agency X doesn't have appropriate openings, she would appreciate your advice during a call or coffee.

If it's okay, I'll e-intro, or you can email her directly at Lisa@email.com.

Thanks,
Michelle

By ghosting this, Lisa makes it super easy for Michelle to just copy and send. Countless times I've seen the email copied word for word.

Ultimately, Michelle will make the intro or she won't, but when it's so much easier, her likelihood increases dramatically.[162]

84

How do I fill out a job application?

Trudy Steinfeld, an expert in recruitment, goes further than most, and claims that it can be worth applying for a job if you have just 60% of the qualifications. She says that job descriptions include everything they can think of, but if they need to train you on 40% of the skills needed, that is acceptable.[163]

Typically, large companies have formal online platforms for applying for jobs. After registering, they guide you through the application process, allow you to save a partially completed application, and track the submissions you've made.

Most large companies use an Applicant Tracking System (ATS) to process applications posted to their websites. As per Lewis Lustman, the ATS can be configured to filter applications based on any number of formulas, for example: "keywords for a job opening, including job skills, former employers, years of experience and schools attended."[164]

Be sure to save your own copy of the job description and your application. It is a best practice to write your response in a word processing application before pasting it into the online application. This will allow you to spell and grammar check it and to avoid being pressured by any time constraints built into the system or "saving" issues. Be sure there are absolutely no spelling or grammatical errors. For many companies, that means an automatic disqualification.

Before you apply to a job, check for connections in the company. If you have connections, or if you were referred to the job through a colleague, be sure to mention their name, after confirming with the reference.

When applying to companies that don't utilize these systems, you may be asked to submit a resume and cover letter to a company email address. Keep track of all your submissions.

Julie is an amazing recruiter with a great depth of knowledge about the process. She suggests the following regarding filling out applications:

> Fill out the information to the best of your ability. If you don't understand the question or not sure, leave blank or type in not applicable. Be honest with your answers, makes sure the dates are correct and don't lie about your present compensation, if you are gainfully employed. Make sure you include any attachments necessary and go back over your application before you submit for accuracy and spelling.[165]

85

What do I do after submitting a job application?

If you applied through an online system, you likely won't know who to contact to check the status. If this is the case, your standard action is to wait. Unless you have a contact in the company, there is not much else you can do. Unfortunately, most companies do not notify you if you're declined. "A recent survey of 56 companies with at least 500 employees found that just 27% have a formal process to decline every external candidate they consider for an opening, reports CareerXroads, a Human Resources consulting firm in Princeton, N.J."[166] Continue with your job search until you sign an employment contract.

If you applied to a job through a referral, contact them to ask when it would be best to follow up. Be sure to act per their directions. If you don't hear from your contact, give them 3-4 business days before sending a gentle reminder. There can be several dynamics at play that cause delays. If you sense the job may be closed—either someone else got the position or the role is no longer needed—get confirmation through a contact in the company.

Following is info from Julie, the expert recruiter, on waiting for a response after submitting your application online:

> Some application technology platforms generate a reply to the applicant right away acknowledging their submission. This at least lets you know that your material was successfully transmitted. There are a fair amount of online application systems that don't acknowledge your information. This is sometime referred to as the "black hole". This can be frustrating especially if they company has a "no phone calls please" policy. A two week wait time can be common for expecting a response either way. There are occasions where you will never hear back and unfortunately never know why you didn't get a response. [167]

86

How do I prepare for the interview?

First, congratulations on making it to this crucial step! Let's ensure you are ready for the challenge. There are four areas of preparation for the job interview. Go into the interview confident by knowing everything you can about the:

1	Company	**3**	Role
2	Interviewer	**4**	Interviewee (You!)

Company

Know the company as if you worked there already. What newsworthy events have been in the press over the last year? Were the stories positive or negative? Were the stories relevant to your position? If so what's your take on the issue?

Do they provide a career section covering what to expect in an interview? If so, study all of it. Know the company's mission and values, the names of the C-suite executives (CEO, CMO, CIO, CTO, COO, CFO), and who the board members are. Imagine you are the CEO. What challenges would you be facing? What successes of the company would you highlight?

If the company publishes an annual report, study it. Understand the company's position in the industry. Is the company growing, condensing, or stable? Be aware of their current challenges. Know the essence of the brand.

Learn what you can about the organizational structure and your department's position in it. What is the status of your department? Is it newly formed? Going through reorganization? Stable? How could your contribution positively influence the success of the department and the company?

Present stories about successes from your career that would be relevant to the company. Use metrics when available. For example, "increased customer base 125% in 2 months", "created successful Facebook campaign resulting in 5,000 new likes," or "developed a new app that improved customer engagement by 35%."

Interviewer

"The interview" is actually a series of interviews. You will start with a screener interview. If you make it past the screener, you will meet with at least the hiring manager. If that interview goes well, it is still not the end of the story. Today, the average interviewee has 14 interviews for one job.[168]

During the interview, be perceptive of non-verbal cues. This is especially important in phone or video-based interviews where you are limited to your visual and auditory senses.

If it's a phone interview, does the interviewer's voice sound tense or distracted? Try to read their emotion through their voice, and adjust accordingly. If they sound agitated, defuse the situation by asking how their day is going. If they seem distracted, draw their focus with a poignant question. Your ability to be empathetic is an easy way to demonstrate one of your soft skills.

Try to discern the greatest deterrent, in the eyes of the interviewer, to hiring you based on their behavior during the interview. Do they seem concerned about your lack of experience? A lack of certain skills? If you have a sense of their concern, ask them to explain, then alleviate their worries. For example, if the concern is a lack of experience, you could mention that you learn fast and are willing to put in extra effort until you get up to speed.

Role

Refer to the original job description. Know the job description inside and out. For every responsibility, write down an example of how you have accomplished that task in the past. Use a "story" format. If you don't have direct experience, describe a similar instance. For example, if you're asked if you know a certain software but don't, describe a similar software you have used and the process you went through to learn it.

Before the interview, use creative visualization. Imagine yourself in this role. What would your challenges be? How would you be successful? Be prepared to answer questions, but also have questions about the role where the job description is vague, contradictory, or suspect.

Interviewee (You!)

Be emotionally, psychologically, and physically prepared for the interview. Success comes from confidence. Confidence comes from security. Security comes from preparation. Study for the interview. All the preparation in the world, however, will mean nothing if you don't express your enthusiasm for the company and the role.

Prepare your "STAR" responses to interview questions. STAR is an acronym for:

- Situation
- Task
- Action
- Result

Document two or three stories that will demonstrate how you'll fulfill the job requirements. Your STAR stories should illustrate how you'll get the job done, even if you don't have all the skills listed in the job description.

In addition, be prepared with at least two intelligent questions for your interviewer. This is your chance to discover the most important questions about your potential employer. Use these questions to determine if the job and the company align with your skills, strengths, personality, and most importantly, your values.

Ask questions about the company, the job, and the department. Some examples are: "What skills are you looking for in an ideal candidate? Why is this position available? How will success be defined at 30/60/90 day intervals?

Practice asking your prepared questions with a friend, in the mirror, and/or on video. Objectively evaluate how you present yourself. Do you seem confident, professional, approachable? Do you have any presentation habits that you could refine such as saying "um" during pauses, jiggling your leg, a giggling nervously, etc.? Would you hire you?

The interview is not an interrogation. Both parties are learning about each other. Be clear on your professional brand and use every opportunity to express it. Don't hesitate to ask the interviewer to clarify a question, to redirect the conversation, to express your knowledge, or to seek more info from the interviewer. Feel free to take notes or bring your prepared questions. It shows you are committed to the process.

Assure your online presence is limited to professional content—nothing you would not want an interviewer to see. Your Facebook, Instagram, LinkedIn, and other publicly accessible online accounts are an extension of you. They will be reviewed by your interviewer before you meet.

Look your best. Wear the appropriate clothing for your industry; don't wear strong perfume/cologne, and make sure your breath smells fresh (no smoke or coffee residue). Someone interviewing for a job waiting tables dresses differently from a Vice President candidate. If you are not sure, err on the side of being overdressed.

Arrive early to the area of the interview. Then, enter the building five to ten minutes before the interview time, depending on how lengthy the building security is and what floor you're going to. If you are unfamiliar with the route to the company or the area, do a dry run before your interview appointment.

Follow the same procedure for every interview. Assure you know what is most important to the person who is interviewing you. Consider their position, what your relationship will be, and how you will best support their success.

After the interview

Allow yourself time at the end of the interview to inquire how it went. Ask if there is anything you could clarify before leaving and what you can expect next. If they are not interested in moving to the next step, they may deliver a vague answer such as, "Someone will be in touch." If you have a sense that a certain answer you provided wasn't received well, address it before leaving.

As soon as possible, and within 24 hours, send a thank you note. Although it may seem obvious, state that you are interested in moving to the next step.

See Anne's advice below on how to be prepared for an interview. Anne is a career coach with a background in recruiting:

> First and foremost, be prepared. That means check out the company's website and read everything. Read their press but also do your own online search of what people are saying about the company and the industry. Look on LinkedIn to see if you know anyone who works there. You could reach out to them before you go in and ask if they have any helpful inside scoop for you. Also, if you know the names of the people you're interviewing with, look them up and familiarize yourself with their backgrounds.
>
> Write down questions that you have about the company or the people you're meeting with. Take note of things of interest such as if one of the hiring managers went to the same college as you did or the company website shows photos of a volunteer day at an organization that you're involved with.
>
> Practice taking an interviewer through your resume and portfolio if you have one. Be prepared for a range of questions from the open ended "Tell me about yourself" to the clichés like "Where do you see yourself in five years?" to the unexpected like "If money were no object, what would be your dream project?"
>
> Practice answers to behavioral type questions like "Tell me about a time when you had someone on your team you didn't like and how did you handle it?"
>
> If there are gaps in your resume, be prepared to explain them. Also, be prepared for the salary question. If it makes you nervous (and believe me, it makes most people nervous) do your research, ask someone you trust for advice and then

practice answering the question. A range is usually best, look them in the eye, say it and then stop talking. People tend to get uncomfortable and continue talking and weaken their position.

Be sure to get a good night's sleep and give yourself enough time to get there, allowing for potential delays. Finally, remember that although it can be nerve wracking to be interviewed, you are also finding out whether you like them and if this opportunity is for you. Think of it as a dialogue rather than a performance.[169]

87
Who will interview me?

The screening interview

When you've been selected for an interview, you will receive a call or an email informing you of a "screening" interview (it may not be referred to as such). The goal of the screening interview is to assure you have the minimal qualifications required and to confirm the validity of the information stated on your resume: job history, skills, education. In addition, a good screener will support you by answering questions you have about the company, the role, or the interview process. (This is more typically the case if the screener is a recruiter.)

Usually, a "screening" interview is conducted over the phone, or possibly through a video chat. If you applied directly to a corporation, you'll most likely be contact by the HR department. If you applied through a recruiter, you'll hear from the recruiter. If you applied to a small company without an HR department, you may not have a screening interview at all. The initial contact will instead focus on when you can schedule an interview with the hiring manager.

You may first get an email asking to schedule a call. In that case, be sure to schedule with enough time to prepare. If you receive a call out of the blue (consider never answering calls for which you don't have a caller ID), ask to reschedule so you have time to prepare.

Although the screening interview will typically not be as intense as the hiring manager interview, if you don't succeed, you won't get any further, so take it seriously. If you are successfully vetted, you will move on to the hiring manager, the person you will report to.

The hiring manager

The interview with the hiring manager will usually be the most rigorous interview you'll experience. This is the person who directly needs your help and knows the role best. Selecting the right candidate means personal success for the hiring manager. Assure that you have good chemistry. Rely on your instincts for that call!

360° interview

Many companies employ a 360° interview process. This involves being interviewed by colleagues that will be your peers, your direct reports (people who you will lead), and senior leaders (department heads, division presidents, or the C-suite, depending on the size of the company).

The concept of a 360° interview is to ensure a better culture fit. It may be hard for you as the interviewee to get a sense of the company culture by meeting one person, but if you meet several, you will have a better sense of the company. In addition, the company will receive multiple perspectives of you from team members with different needs.

In these interviews, try to assess, or learn beforehand, what the relationships are among the interviewers, what is going on in their departments, and any critical issues that would be relevant to your role. Stay neutral in any areas of conflict. Assess what is important to each stakeholder for your role, and address their concerns. Express a willingness to work as part of the team!

88

What questions should I expect in the interview?

What questions will be asked?

The questions asked in an interview will vary with the role, the skill of the interviewer, and the interviewing best practices of the company. Many people are not adept at interviewing, especially since they don't do it frequently. They may resort to a standard set of questions which won't provide them with the best information.

Regardless of their ability, your goal is to present yourself in the best light. Answer each question fully and clearly. Be prepared with an answer the following common questions (and search online to find more):

1 What is your greatest strength?
2 What is your greatest weakness?
3 Tell me about yourself.
4 Why should we hire you?
5 What are your salary expectations?
6 Why are you leaving or have you left your job?
7 Why do you want this job?
8 How do you handle stress and pressure?
9 Describe a difficult work situation/project and how you overcame it.
10 What are your goals for the future?[170]

Be liberal with your interpretation of the questions. You can politely redirect through humor or transition to an example that better illustrates your capabilities.

Imagine that you're asked question eight, "How do you handle stress and pressure?" What does that imply? That the job is very stressful and demanding? Your retort may be, "Is this job known to be stressful? What is the source of the stress? Are others on the team affected?" Use the questions to learn more about the job, the company, and the interviewer as well. You are deciding if this job is right for you!

Pull your answers from real job experiences, and relay them in the form of stories with beginnings, middles, and ends. If you are a student or recent graduate, use your experience from internships or volunteer work if you don't have relevant work experience. Start with your most poignant stories, and imagine how you could use them as answers. Write down your answers to all the questions you imagine will be asked. You can also videotape your responses to refine your presentation.

Let's use question nine above as an example of how the dialog may proceed.

Interviewer: Could you describe how you overcame a difficult situation while working on a project?

Interviewee:
<Include the question in your answer>
While working on a new project, I encountered a difficult situation regarding the team dynamics.
<Story beginning—set the stage>
The company needed to redesign their highest revenue generating digital product which served several divisions across the globe.
<Story middle—the conflict>
Each division was anxious to assure that their requirements were met. The divisions with the largest budget were dominating the discussions which caused tension.
<Story ending—resolution>
I suggested implementing an objective requirements evaluation scale which assured the common requirements for all

divisions would be funded. Unique requirements would be covered by the division requesting it.

<Summarize your skill and use metrics if relevant>

Through analyzing the team dynamics and implementing an equitable alternative, the project requirements were completed in half the time.

<Confirmation>

Is that the type of example you were looking for?

What questions should I ask?

The interview is not a one-way street. You are participating in the interview to ensure the job is right for you based on the tasks, relationships, current opportunities, and definition of success. To find out if it's a good fit, you may ask the following questions:

1 What skills and experiences would make an ideal candidate?
2 What is the single largest problem facing your staff?
3 What have you enjoyed most about working here?
4 What constitutes success at this position and this firm?
5 Do you have any hesitations about my qualifications?
6 Do you offer continuing education and professional training?
7 Can you tell me about the team I'll be working on?
8 What can you tell me about your new products or plans for growth?
9 Who previously held this position?
10 What is the next step in the process?[171]

What questions cannot be asked?

When you are in an interview, most people's inclination will be to answer all questions from the interviewer. However, whether intentionally or not, interviewers may ask questions that are illegal to ask. As per Vivian Giang, "State and federal laws make discrimination based on certain protected categories, such as national origin, citizenship, age, marital status, disabilities, arrest and conviction record, military discharge status, race, gender, or pregnancy status, illegal."[172] Questions may seem appropriate within the context of the interview, but your answers could be used prejudicially against you. If you were asked if you have any children and replied "no," the next question could be, "Do you plan on having children?" If you said yes, the company could decide not to hire to avoid paying for your maternity leave.

"If you are asked any inappropriate questions, [it is best] not to lie, but, instead, politely decline to answer."[173] Familiarize yourself with the nuances of these legalities in your state. Also, consider indirect ways you might be asked an illegal question. They might ask if you remember experiencing a certain historic event and how old you were at that time, which would divulge your current age. You can answer these questions, of course, but consider what that means about the company and your relationship with it.

89

I received a job offer, now what?

Well, congratulations! You'll probably be notified of your job offer by a phone call from the HR department. In the case of a small company, you may hear directly from the hiring manager or someone in senior leadership.

Keep in mind that you are not expected to provide an immediate response. Even if you are very excited and this is your dream job, pause to ensure all is in order. Don't feel that you must take the first offer, but let the HR associate know you are excited and thankful.

Ask when you'll receive the official written offer, which can be delivered digitally through an online portal, secure email or in paper form. The official offer is typically a set of documents that require your review and signature. Confirm that everything you discussed regarding salary, benefits, hours, location, etc. are correctly documented before signing and officially accepting.

If you are unsure about accepting a job, take steps to evaluate the opportunity:

1   Review the objectives for this job as compared to your long-term goals as defined during your self-awareness explorations.
2   Write down the pros and cons of the job to quantify your perceptions. Consider the day-to-day experience, the compensation offered, and the potential opportunities.
3   Talk to your advisory board. This is your group of close friends and associates who have your best interest in mind.

Anne, a career coach with a background in recruiting, provides us with a look at what happens when you receive a job offer.

Usually you will get a verbal offer. Hopefully they will give you all the information you need, but if not, feel free to ask questions. You should know the salary, title, benefits, who you report to, when they want you to start.

Most people won't expect an answer on the spot. If you know you want to accept, ask for time to think it over and suggest that you call in the morning, or ask "when would be a good time to call tomorrow?"

If it's a Friday, you can usually request the weekend to think about it. If the number is lower than you hoped for, ask if there's any flexibility on the salary. No matter their answer, you can still come back with a counter offer. But if you're happy with the salary, don't counter offer just to do it. I've had people do that who later told me they thought they were supposed to and after I had worked hard to get them the best salary we could do, I found it off putting.

If you have another offer coming in, then ask for a few more days, but be specific as in "Could I have until Friday to give you my answer?" Or you could say "I am expecting another offer; how long could you give me to make my decision?" They won't be thrilled but if you want to see what this other offer is, then see if you can get it. But you'll have to get it quickly and if you can't, don't expect the place that made the offer to wait longer than a week.

You can also ask for something in writing before you've given them an answer. Then once you've accepted, the next thing to discuss is start date. Then you will sign the offer letter and return it. If you end up declining, do it graciously and follow up with a thank you and "best of luck to you" email.[174]

90

What do I do after I accept a job offer?

Be sure to follow proper procedures and act with professionalism after you receive a job offer. Once you have made your decision and communicated your acceptance of the offer, follow these steps:

1   **INFORM OTHER PROSPECTIVE EMPLOYERS THAT YOU HAVE ACCEPTED AN OFFER.** If you were in the process of interviewing with other companies, inform them in an email that you accepted another offer. Thank them for their time and keep the door open for future opportunities.

2   **ADHERE TO INSTRUCTIONS AND COMMUNICATE WITH YOUR CONTACT AS SCHEDULED.** Deliver requested information promptly, and schedule required drug testing. Sometimes, jobs may take a long time to process a new hire. The HR department could be very busy hiring a new wave of employees, they may have to replace a senior leader before hiring you, or there could be other complications. Be patient and follow the defined protocol.

3   **KEEP YOUR FOCUS.** You are in a vulnerable position before you are officially hired. Anecdotal evidence suggests that about 1 in 20 offers are rescinded during this stage.[175] This can be due to inappropriate behavior after the offer—social media comments, email responses, comments to other employees, etc. This could also occur because of miscommunications in the verbal agreements.

4   **DON'T OFFICIALLY ANNOUNCE YOUR NEW JOB UNTIL ALL PAPERS ARE SIGNED.** After you feel secure in your new role, you can update your status on LinkedIn and other channels.

91

How do I manage multiple offers?

If you receive an offer, inform other potential employers if you've reached the interview stage or if you'd like a counter offer. Never lie and state that you have an offer when you don't as a negotiation tactic.

Use the same strategies for deciding if a job is the right fit when deciding among multiple offers. Be sure to consider your overall career path. Which job will take you on the career path you planned? Don't be swayed by perks, bonuses, or other "temporary" incentives. Stick to your goals.

What if one of your potential employers asks about what other offers you have received? You're not obligated to provide any details. You may mention something that is attracting you to a different job offer as a bargaining tactic, but in most cases the less you say, the better.

92
How do I reject an offer?

If you decide not to pursue an offer, inform the potential employer. Communicate this in written form. If you have a specific reason, present it in a positive and professional manner. Sometimes, you may like the company, but not the role offered. Be sure to mention that, and express your interest in future opportunities. If you know someone else who may want the role, ask if they are open to your recommendations.

93

How do I assess my "value" to my employer?

How do you know how much you are worth to your employer? This is the first question to answer before beginning a negotiation. Several factors create the "value recipe":

- **EXPERIENCE**—For how long and at what level of intensity have you been practicing your skills?
- **EXPERTISE**—What is your depth of knowledge and ability to express that knowledge in real-life situations?
- **MARKETPLACE**—What is the state of the global political and economic climate for your industry? Is the marketplace flooded with, or in need of, people with your skill set?
- **SOFT SKILLS**—How are your people skills—managing direct reports, communicating up to senior leadership, serving as a positive influence for the company, etc.?
- **ACCESSIBILITY**—Do you live close by the office? Are you available in emergencies? Can you work flexible hours if needed?

The higher you rank yourself on these dimensions, the more valuable you are to your employer. Then, find out what the market rate for your role is in your zip code:

- Conduct an online job search for your role.
- Check websites such as PayScale, Glassdoor, and SalaryScout. These sites aggregate user-driven data to provide examples of salaries and real-life experiences.

- The National Association of Colleges and Employers (NACE) salary calculator can provide a salary estimate based on your location.

Whether you are hired in a salaried position or run your own business, you'll earn less money when you start, simply because it will take you longer to do everything. Over time, you'll develop techniques and experience to improve your efficiently. Then your compensation will increase. Strive for the optimal way of accomplishing any given task. This will keep your mind sharp, engaged and ahead of the competition!

94
How do I negotiate my employment contract?

Whether you negotiate your employment offer is up to you. The best way to be successful is to be prepared and confident. You were offered a job, so you know that the company wants you. Express interest and excitement about the job. Make sure the employer knows you are interested in working for them before negotiating.

Arm yourself with the following information:

- Average, high, and low salaries for your position in your location
- Average, high, and low salaries for your position in the company (if available)
- What is the lowest salary you are willing to accept and still feel good about the position? Present this as the bottom end of a salary range that you would accept. The amount should be realistic and based on the budget you need for your living expenses.
- What other benefits are negotiable—vacation time, ability to set hours, tuition or other training benefits such as conferences, enhanced health benefits, etc.?

If the employer asks you what your acceptable range is, either toss the question back to them, or present them with the range you've researched, and ask if that is aligned with their offer.

As an added incentive, remember that salary increases are based on a percentage of your salary. A higher starting salary means that your raises will be based on a larger figure.

Counter offer letter template

Dear [HR Associate, Hiring Manager]:

As per our phone call today, thank you for your time discussing the job offer for [Job Title] at [Company Name]. I am very excited about the prospect of working for [Company Name], but as discussed today, I hope we can negotiate a modified compensation package.

Based on my research, the role of [Job Title] commands a maximum salary of [$$] in [city of job location.] I believe that based on my experience, [$$] would be a fair salary. In addition, I am requesting compensation for [conference name]. I typically attend the [conference name] each year to keep informed of industry trends and best practices. I would also like you to consider adding [This could be tuition reimbursement, vacation days, healthcare or an enhancement to any other benefit offered].

I greatly appreciate your time and consideration to my request.

Please contact me if you need any clarification.

Thank you again for this opportunity.

Sincerely,
[Your Name]
[email address]
[phone number]
[mailing address]

95
What about legalities: background check, drug test...?

After you have accepted your offer and negotiated the salary and benefits, it's time for legalities. At least, this is usually the case in most large corporations. Smaller companies and startups, or companies in certain industries, may not require drug tests, but today most companies will conduct a background check.

There isn't anything you need to do for the background check except sign an approval form. For the companies that require a drug test, it is typically mandatory. You'll schedule an appointment as a designated lab, and submit a urine sample for testing. In some cases, where sobriety is a significant liability, such as in law enforcement or other instances where lives could be at stake, there may be more extensive testing, such as hair follicles or blood test. Results are submitted directly to HR, and you will be notified of the results.

Success in Your Role

You worked hard to get your new job. Now it's time to shift gears and ensure that you are successful in this new role. What does it take to be successful? Let's find out!

96
What Is entailed with "onboarding?"

Onboarding is the process of providing you with all the information and materials required for your job. Someone on your team, or several people, will manage the different aspects of the onboarding process.

Administrator: Directs you to your work location, stocks it with office supplies, your business cards, phone, etc.

Tech Admin: Supplies a computer, intranet IDs, email and related services.

HR: HR intranet login assigned for access to career-related info, administrative forms for healthcare, financial benefits, employee handbooks, and direct deposit instructions.

Hiring Manager: Team introductions, organizational chart, detailed responsibilities, assessment procedure, meeting protocols/acronyms.

Following is a checklist of the basics:

- Start date and time
- Normal work hours
- Procedures for working off-site
- Payment schedule
- Dress code
- Office address
- Hiring Manager contact info
- Usual lunch/break hours and lengths
- Time tracking or related reporting
- Use of email, phone, and meeting rooms
- Scheduling of time off and vacation days
- Management of expenses
- Key contact people
- Emergency exit procedures

Cindy is an HR expert who has worked in Fortune 500 companies. Following is her description of onboarding:

Onboarding is the process used to orient you to the company. Sometimes the company will send you materials to read/watch prior to your start date. Typically, a schedule of meetings with individuals you will be working with will be scheduled for you over your first few days.

Onboarding often has a compliance component in which you will be expected to review and acknowledge of the employee handbook, take required training such as Sexual Harassment Prevention training. Some companies assign a mentor or buddy to work with a new hire. Onboarding can last from a few hours up to a few months depending on how formal the program is.[176]

97

How do I prepare for my first day of work?

Cindy, an HR expert, provides direction for your first day of work:

> To prepare for your first day of work, take a longer-term view and think about the first 90 days. There are many articles published on what to focus on during your first 90 days. Often missed is the importance of finding out how your manager prefers to communicate. Do they prefer formal weekly meetings or do they prefer email communication or to have you stop by with a question?[177]

98

What criteria contribute to my success on the job?

In a nutshell, there are three criteria that contribute to your success:

Knowledge

1 Expertise in your job responsibilities
2 Ongoing improvement and expansion of your hard and soft skills
3 Informed about your company: leadership objectives, organizational structure, values, internal politics, status in the industry

Behavior

1 Seek opportunities to advance your leadership skills and go beyond your job description
2 Exude confidence and don't hesitate to ask questions
3 Be goal-oriented, and log your accomplishments
4 Observe and learn from top performers
5 Express your brand

Relationship management

1 Participate in networking groups on the job and in organizations outside of the job
2 Engage with your advisors, mentors, and professional network
3 Support your leaders and co-workers

99

What are communication best practices?

Communication is the exchange of information between two or more people. To ensure that exchange is productive, utilize all your senses to process the information: listen to words and tone, observe facial expressions and gestures, and sense emotions.

Miscommunication occurs when we move away from our sense-based observations to assumptions. Then, our imagination reigns and we rely on fiction instead of facts.

Steve Gaffney, author and speaker, refers to this fact/fiction dichotomy as "notice" versus "imagine." He explains how this communication phenomenon works:

> The most critical strategy for honestly communicating and working effectively with anyone is simple, yet it is the key to resolving the most difficult problems in less time and with greater skill. It is the distinction between what we "notice" and what we "imagine." I was first introduced to this concept by Dr. Brad Blanton...
>
> For our purposes, the word "notice" refers to the facts of the situation, and the word "imagine" refers to everything else that goes on in our heads — our opinions, assumptions, and judgments. [For example:] You notice that someone has on a red tie, and you imagine that the tie is fashionable. Someone else might notice the tie, but imagine it is not fashionable. You notice someone came in 30 minutes late to the staff meeting, and you may imagine that the person just forgot about the meeting. Someone else might notice that the person came in 30 minutes late and imagine that he doesn't care about the meeting.[178]

The best way to remedy this situation is to continually check in to confirm that what you think you observed or heard is what the other person intended. The good news is that most anyone can learn this "reaffirming" habit. You don't have to be born a great communicator. You can evolve into one.

Five points to keep in mind for good communications:

1 **PREPARATION**: Come prepared with the facts.
2 **OPEN MINDEDNESS**: Don't let your filters or prejudices obstruct the truth.
3 **ENGAGEMENT**: Be present, and activate all your senses.
4 **THE UNSAID**: Be alert for what is missing.
5 **CONFIRMATION**: Validate info received during the exchange.

These points are self-explanatory, but number four could benefit from an example. When meeting clients to kick off new design projects, I have found it critical to not let the client dictate the discussion because too much is left unsaid. Following is a very typical dialog:

> **CLIENT:** We need a website. Can you create one for us that looks like this website? How much is it going to cost?
> **ME:** Sure, but what results are you expecting from the website?
> **CLIENT:** Everyone has a website, so we need one.
> **ME:** Yes, that is true, but websites can provide a myriad of functions, be developed with a wide range of complexity, and require various levels of maintenance. My job is to help you understand what the right parameters are for your company.
> **CLIENT:** Oh. I don't know.
> **ME:** No problem. Let's start at the beginning. Tell me the story of your company...

From experience, I know that my clients often don't know what they don't know. As a professional, it is my job to know that, and to know how to get the information I needed to build a successful website.

100
How can I optimize my relationship with a manager?

Your manager is your leader. As a leader, they should ideally provide you with guidance regarding your responsibilities, support your career advancement, and help you navigate the company hierarchy. They should ensure that your group/department/division works cohesively towards shared goals. However, there may be circumstances which prevent the ideal version of that relationship. You may have a personality clash with your manager. Your manager may not be well trained as a leader. There a multiplicity of factors that hamper the relationship.

Regardless of the reason for the problems, take steps to improve the relationship. First, try to better understand your manager by asking yourself these questions:

1 What drives your leader?
2 What are your leader's goals?
3 What are your leader's challenges?
4 Notice your leader's relationship with others; how do those relationships differ from your relationships?
5 What causes friction between you?
6 How does your leader prefer to communicate (in-person, email, phone etc.)?
7 What's is your leader's management style, and how can you help facilitate that? Could you contribute to weekly updates, emails, goals & accomplishment meetings, etc.?

Second, with a better understanding of your manager, consider what you could do to stay in sync. Note your work styles. For example, if you leader values punctuality, and you regularly arrive ten minutes late, start ensuring you are early. If your leader is a micromanager, but you need a lot of space, consider how you might meet in the middle.

That brings us to point number three. Communicate about any discrepancies between your expectations at the time of the occurrence. Do not wait for an official status meeting. Make sure you have regular check-ins, but when issues arise, point them out right away. If you are having a problem that affects others, notify your leader. Don't let your leader hear it from someone else.

Lastly, if your efforts have not resulted in any progress, and the ongoing issues could affect your review and your progress, document them. If need be, bring it to the attention of an Ombudsman (they investigate complaints from employees) or someone in the HR department. You should not have to endure unprofessional or abusive behavior.

101
How do I ask for feedback from my manager?

Not everyone in a managerial position has received proper training for how to manage their direct reports. Even if they have, not every manager is comfortable with assessing and delivering feedback. It is also true that not everyone can accept feedback. Remember to be open and listen while feedback is being delivered. Take the initiative to kick start a feedback loop that will maximize your career goals and support your manager in their goals.

Ask for feedback in a face-to-face meeting with your manager and suggest creating a framework for how you can receive feedback. Include the following:

TIMEFRAME—Receiving feedback in the moment has been shown to be most effective. However, depending on your manager's schedule, that may not always be possible. Be sure to schedule at least a 15-minute weekly meeting to receive feedback along with other updates. The recurring meeting could be extended or cancelled as needed.

COMMUNICATION STYLE—Communication style is how you convey information using language and is determined by your age, gender, location and other factors. Take the time to research this topic and understand your communication style. For example, one dimension of communication style is the level of directness. Your manager may be very direct and prefer to send you a bulleted list before your meeting. You may prefer that your manager gently deliver feedback as part of conversation. Discuss a compromise that considers both of your styles.

CAREER GOALS—You'll want feedback that supports your career goals in areas that you'd like to grow. Ensure your manager delivers feedback relevant to your goals. For example, if your next role will include management, ask for feedback on how you work with others on the team, suggestions for classes or reading, or opportunities to manage on a test project.

THE MESSAGE—It's best to leave the content of the feedback to your manager, but expect it to be about skills, communications, behaviors and project results. Feedback can address successes or note areas for improvement.

FOLLOW UP—It is your responsibility to keep track of the feedback you've received and improve where necessary. When you've made an improvement, ask your manager if they've noticed a change. Everyone likes to see progress, but we can only defined progress if we are measuring the change.

102

How can I optimize my relationship with a direct report?

The same three core principles discussed for optimizing your relationship with a manager apply to direct reports—the employees that report to you. It is up to you to support and motivate your direct reports and produce results that support the company's goals.

Results of a Gallup survey on manager-employee engagement reveal that "among employees who strongly agree that their manager helps them set performance goals, 69 percent are engaged. When employees strongly disagree, just 8 percent are engaged, while 53 percent are actively disengaged," per Jim Harter and Amy Adkins in a 2015 article from the *Gallup Business Journal.*[179]

The following three points are most important when managing a team:

1 **COMMUNICATE**: Listen, perceive the unspoken, be concise and transparent
2 **SUPPORT**: Lead without dictating, instill trust, facilitate teamwork
3 **GROW**: Inspire excellence, value and nourish expertise, recognize and correct knowledge/behavior gaps

103

How is my performance evaluated?

Each company has a specific process for evaluating performance, and the results could affect your annual bonus (if your company offers a bonus) and your opportunities for advancement. The traditional approach, which has been used predominantly since the 1970's is as follows:

1   Senior leadership sets high level goals for the company.
2   These goals are cascaded down through the ranks, and you, with the support of your leader, determine your goals for the year. The goals are typically in the form of KPIs (Key Performance Indicators) which are metrics or behaviors that can be measured.
3   Your performance is tracked against these KPIs, with a final tally during an annual review.
4   At year's end, your success in achieving these goals is evaluated. In some cases, this evaluation includes input from your leader, peers, vendors, and others that you've worked with for a 360° evaluation. Other times, it may be solely from your supervisor.
5   Your annual bonus and possibility for advancement are determined by the results of your annual review.

Recently, however, there has been a backlash against this formal review process. Because of the sheer dislike of the process by most employees, and the amount of time it takes, companies have been rethinking the value of the performance review and how it can be restructured to better produce employee growth, performance, and retention.

A recent article in the Harvard Business Review investigates this exploration of an alternative solution for performance reviews. The crux of the problem is that performance reviews "hold people accountable for past behavior at the expense of improving current performance and grooming talent for the future, both of which are critical for organizations' long-term survival."[180] The new method emphasizes feedback in the moment, as opposed to waiting for the end of the year, and deemphasizing numbers-based evaluation. With immediate feedback from supervisors and peers, provided in person or through an app, a better training opportunity is created. This results in growth, as opposed to a punitive, backwards-looking system. The article states that it's estimated "that about 70% of multinational companies are moving toward this model, even if they haven't arrived quite yet."[181]

The bottom line is make sure you are clear on the system your company is using. If they use a traditional method, it doesn't mean that you and your supervisor can't agree to work on a way of including immediate feedback. Regardless of the formal system for performance growth, manage your own growth in the way most valuable to you. This should include documentation of the learning opportunities offered by your supervisor, colleagues, and vendors.

104
What are employee networks?

Employee networks, also called affinity groups, are social subgroups within large corporations. These networks are formed based on common interests, such as gender, sexual orientation, religion, or ethnicity. An employee network can serve several functions:

- Provides a safe space and facilitates orientation to the organization
- Serves as a medium to communicate issues experienced by that group to senior leadership
- Facilitates talent acquisition by offering the prospect of support from the network to prospective employees
- Delivers a broader understanding of target markets that share characteristics with the employee networks
- Educates the employee base about the experience of those in the employee networks

Employee networks (ENs) will conduct various initiatives within an organization which can range from networking events outside of work hours to in-office happy hours or luncheons designed to unite different groups. ENs can provide support for related nonprofits. For example, our LGBTQ network at a Fortune 100 company asked all members to volunteer at events for one of the three nonprofits we supported. We also developed a campaign to reach out to our company's customers who are within our demographic as part of a larger company initiative. The result was an increase in revenue in those markets.

One excellent example of the strength of employee networks is success of LGBTQ networks. These networks across the nation have worked to educate fellow employees about equal rights considerations for LGBTQ employees. This was exemplified in the issue of marriage equality. The grassroots support for marriage equality in corporate employee networks helped drive the change in federal law.

105
How can I get promoted?

From day one of your new job, understand the requirements for a promotion. Many companies expect you to be doing the 'promotion' job before they will give you the title. To demonstrate your capabilities, ask to take on more responsibilities. Understand the structure of the company; not all companies have upward mobility options if they are 'flat organizations.' In that case, you might receive financial increases, but never change your title. Consider that more money doesn't increase job satisfaction; job content does.

Following are some general guidelines, but communicate with your supervisor leader to understand what is most valued in your company and what you need to do in your role to be promoted.

The behaviors

- **BE AN EXPERT**—Execute your responsibilities as an expert in your job. Stay informed on changes in your field.
- **BE A PROBLEM-SOLVER**—Some organizations can be very bureaucratic which can create roadblocks to success. Figure out how to work within the system (or outside of it) to get the job done.
- **GO BEYOND THE BASELINE**—Take on work outside of your responsibilities. That may mean finding a special project for another department that could use your expertise or leading a network group.
- **DOCUMENT YOUR ACHIEVEMENTS**—No one knows what you do every day but you. Keep an ongoing list of your achievements, preferably with metrics.

- **PROMOTE YOUR ACHIEVEMENTS**—It's great to keep the achievements list, but it means nothing if it's just on your computer! Be sure to share, and promote your achievements as relevant. Is there a company newsletter, townhall, or other avenue where you could promote your achievements? Could you distribute a report, hold a panel on a topic of your expertise, or speak at a conference?
- **BUILD RELATIONSHIPS**—Promoting your achievements isn't possible if you don't know anyone. You do not work in a vacuum. You're on a team. Develop a support team on the job that includes mentors, coworkers (within your team and outside of your team), and relationships with the senior leadership team (as much as possible).
- **TREAT COWORKERS RESPECTFULLY**—You are not going to love everyone in your company, but you can do your best to treat everyone respectfully. You never know how situations or relationships may change.
- **ASK FOR HELP**—No one knows everything. Know who to ask for help and when. Make sure you assess when it makes sense to ask for help. If it's a question that you can answer in a Google search, don't bother a coworker. If it's a problem that would take you a half day to solve, but you know you someone that could answer it in one minute, then ask! When you do ask, remember the answer or write it down so you don't have to ask again.
- **PARTICIPATE IN AFTER WORK EVENTS**—Socializing with your coworkers, although not a written requirement, is part of success in your job. Events may be formally constructed or spontaneous and casual. Be professional, and enjoy! It is through social events that you learn about people and deepen relationships.

The ask

It may happen that, out of the blue, your leader gives you a promotion, but that is unlikely. If you want a promotion, it will probably come from your intention and planning. Work with your leader from the beginning of the year to work towards a promotion. Have a title in mind for your promotion? Research what is missing from your skill set and experience for the new role. Work with those above you to find opportunities to fill the gaps. Keep track of your progress throughout the year.

106

How should I select the best seminars and conferences?

Through seminars and conferences, you to learn new skills, get industry information, and network. However, there can be an overwhelming number of seminars and conferences to choose from each year. How do you decide which to attend? There are three criteria to consider:

1. Which are the most respected and influential events in your industry?
2. Which events are most relevant to your current needs (skills, networking, industry trends)?
3. What are your budget parameters?

If your company pays for your attendance, research and submit a budget in accordance with your team's procedure to ensure it will be covered by the budget. If you are covering the costs yourself, try to select the best local events to keep expenses low.

107
How do I become an expert?

An expert is someone who has a "special skill or knowledge derived from training or experience."[182] Becoming an expert will provide you with the best opportunity for success and career satisfaction. How do you become an expert? It takes a conscious effort over time, commitment, and a maximization of your most unique and market-relevant skills.

Consider the upcoming evolution towards AI and automation when you choose your specific area of expertise. What expertise will have the longest "shelf life?" Focus on an expertise that is uniquely human, areas that rely on cognition, involve emotional intelligence, and engage/lead people.

Cognitive Psychologist Anders Ericsson studied how experts acquire world-class skills. They are attained by what he calls "deliberate practice," in which stretch goals are used to improve specific weaknesses. It's not just doing the same thing over and over. It's consciously practicing with a feedback loop that allows you to recognize what you're doing wrong and correct it. You improve by attaining the knowledge AND practicing/honing the skill. Measuring improvement through testing is a critical step that is frequently overlooked. How do you know if you are improving if you don't measure?

Ericsson emphasizes that traits we like to refer to as innate gifts are actually hard work. He states that for experts, it is "dedicated training that drives changes in the brain... that make it possible for them to do things that they otherwise could not."[183]

I can tell you that I am not a "naturally" good writer. In fact, I received a "D" on the first paper I wrote in graduate school because of my poor writing skills! I literally did not know how to construct a paragraph. I improved my writing over time by writing longer pieces, consciously expanding my vocabulary, tracking how long it took me to write, and writing on a schedule. I also enlisted expert writers to provide feedback on my work, performed at poetry readings (where I was sometimes booed!), took writing classes, and examined the work of great writers. Over time, improvement came, but if you told me in my first year of grad school that I would someday write a book, I would have assured you, "That will never happen!"

108
What makes a great leader?

You don't have to be a leader to be self-aware, but you certainly should be self-aware to be a leader. If you don't know yourself, it's unlikely you'll be able to lead others.

What makes a great leader? Let's start with what it means to lead. Leading can mean directing the people under your guidance, but it also means seeing the world in a way that resonates with others and being able to communicate that vision. Being a leader on a large scale—that is, with a global impact—comes from knowing yourself, humanity, and the time you live in.

Is a leader born or made? This is an age-old question, but recent research answers the question with tangible proof. Leaders are, in fact, born and made. Per Erika Andersen, the development of leaders follows a bell curve. About 10-15% of people will never become leaders. A roughly equal percentage are naturally born leaders. The remaining ~70% can be trained to be great leaders.[184] That is the majority, so if you must make a guess, assume someone under your leadership can learn to be a great leader.

A leader is:

- **PASSIONATE**—Believes deeply in the issue, company, cause, or group in which they are leading others. For example, Brandon Stanton created Humans of New York—portraits and quotes from New Yorkers—after leaving a bond trader job and finding his passion in photography. He has over 18 million Facebook followers.[185]
- **RESPONSIBLE**—Makes decisions that impact others and is comfortable owning the outcome. Pope Francis knows his words are heard by at least the 1.2 billion Catholics in the world.[186]

- **INSPIRATIONAL**—Communicates their passion to others and drives them to participate. Billie Jean King's advocacy for women in sports led to Title IX, a law that requires equal funding for women's sports in schools, which triggered an increase from 3% to 40% female participation in athletics.[187]
- **VISIONARY**—Imagines the world in a new way that engages others. For example, Steve Jobs believed in the economic and experiential value of innovative product design and demonstrated his vision to the world.
- **BRAVE**—Strength to withstand negative consequences of their beliefs. Mao Hengfeng survived solitary confinement in her native China, but continues "fighting for the right of women in China not to be forced into having an abortion, and for defending rights for people who have been illegally evicted from their homes."[188]

Following are insights from Ann Mehl about leadership:

In my work as an executive coach, I will often gather and present written 360-degree feedback on business leaders at all levels. For people on the receiving end, it can be very difficult to not react negatively or defensively. They may even resort to name calling, which feels good in the moment, but only serves to create more distance and misunderstanding. I encourage my clients to counter this natural instinct by remaining open and curious. Curiosity invites dialogue, which can lead to some useful new insights. I ask them to be *compassionate* with themselves and with those offering the feedback. Both require taking risks. Effective leadership demands that we avoid shutting down, drawing up the battle lines between US and THEM.

Another key foundation of great leadership is the ability to recognize and check our own bias. In order not to demonize the "other", in order not to *weaponize* our contempt, we need to keep a close check on our own worst instinct which is to point the finger of blame. It is a universal truth that what we criticize most harshly in others is the thing we like least about ourselves. What I hate most about you, may be the very thing I hate most about myself.

All great religious and political leaders from history share this unique ability: they strive first to understand the other's problem, before seeking out the common ground. They are (or have trained themselves to be) intensely interested in the viewpoints, ideas, and critiques of their peers. Of course, we can't all be Nelson Mandela, but maybe we can try to understand the "other" point of view without resorting to questioning their intellect or moral integrity.

I think the biggest enemy of people who want to make the world a better place is not liberalism or conservatism, it's cynicism. Our own cynicism that says nothing will ever change and the world is going to hell in a handbasket. I think that's the *real* enemy, and the one we must guard against. It may sound very "Kumbaya," but I sincerely believe that deep down we all want the same thing: a feeling of connectedness with others, to live with hope, peace and security. We just have different ideas about how this can be achieved. Shadowboxing an ugly caricature will not help. As the old saying goes, "If you want to change the world, try starting with yourself."[189]

Transitioning to Your Next Job

Most likely, every job you have will eventually come to an end. The process will start over again. But you will be different. You'll have more experience, more skills, more insights and maybe many other "mores." You may be clearer on what is most important to you. Whenever that moment comes, be open to recognizing it and welcoming it.

109

How do I know when to look for another job?

Succeeding in the current workforce means being comfortable leaving or losing jobs. Those "born in the latter years of the baby boom (1957-1964) held 11.7 jobs from age 18 to age 48."[190]

Another jump in the number of lifetime jobs is happening. "Ninety-one percent of Millennials (born between 1977-1997) expect to stay in a job for less than three years, per the Future Workplace 'Multiple Generations @ Work' survey of 1,189 employees and 150 managers. That means they would have 15-20 jobs over the course of their working lives!"[191]

What are the signs that it's time to look for another job, aside from the three-year mark?

- **NEED A NEW CHALLENGE**—You've achieved mastery in your current position and are ready to expand your repertoire.
- **MINIMAL GROWTH OPPORTUNITIES**—Due to any number of factors outside of your control—industry downturn, unsupportive management, company restructuring—your goals for promotion do not seem within reach.
- **NEGATIVE EXPERIENCES**—Changes in company management (or a merger), values, structure, or location mean that your job no longer amounts to a positive day-to-day experience.
- **EXPLORING A CAREER CHANGE**—You've evolved new interests and skills, and want to investigate career change opportunities.
- **LIFE CHANGES**—You may have to relocate for a spouse or to care for a family member, or you may have health issues that impede your performance in your current job.

Loop back to the start of this book and re-read the self-awareness, relationship building, and intelligence gathering stages before launching your search.

Kelin, a career coach for a top firm, has the following advice on searching for your next opportunity:

> The first rule of thumb is "it's MUCH easier to find a job when you have a job," so never quit your job until you've landed that next role. Another thing to remember is that before you 'jump ship' on your current company do some research and due diligence to see if there are either other jobs within your company or even ways to turn your current role into the dream job that you're looking for. Most companies don't want to lose good employees—it costs them more to hire someone new and, as well, there is a "brain drain" to the company when they lose employees that they'd prefer to keep. So, before you decide to leave your current role try sitting with your manager to see if together you can change/alter your current role to do more of the things you like to do. However, come to the table with a clear idea and the ability to articulate what you'd like to do in specific detail. That way together you can make identify what that new role would be. Be patient with the process but many times it's the best solution.
>
> If you've tried plan A and that doesn't work—then maybe, it's time to start looking outside your current company. However, remember that the saying "the grass is always greener" can sometimes be the reality of job hunting. So, make a list of all the aspects of your future career opportunity that you MUST HAVE—but be realistic. You need to assess your current skills and marketability as well as the current state of the job market in your area.

Many people change jobs because they think that is the best way to make more money—and in some cases, that can be true. However, know that from many years of research, it's shown that money is the not the most important factor that leads to overall job satisfaction. Job content and autonomy, as well as feelings of purpose and connection to the company and other employees, is more important.

Employees find job satisfaction when their values are being met through their work. So, if you are ready to branch out and seek other jobs, make sure you spend some time getting clear on what your work/life values are and how they can be met with your career. For instance, if family time is the most important value to you then taking a job that involves 90% travel is not going to be a good match. If flexibility is most important, then make sure that you can find that life/work balance in your next role.[192]

110
What should I know about leaving a job?

There will come a point in your career where you will leave a job. You may leave the job of your own volition; you may be terminated or laid off. In any case, the most important thing to keep in mind when leaving a job is that everyone you've worked with there will know about it. That means, in keeping with the professionalism of your brand, leave the job in honorable way. Following are the do's and don'ts:

Don't...

- Create a scene of any kind in the office, in an email, or on social media upon your departure.
- Announce a new job until you are officially working there.
- Breach your contract with your employer (for example, by working for a competitor if you have signed a non-compete agreement).

Do...

- Give two weeks' notice.
- Close out all your projects and provide documentation of projects that will be relevant to your successor.
- Write a tasteful and thankful goodbye email.
- Update LinkedIn and make the effort to let your former coworkers know about your new job, as soon as it is secured.

If you leave a job because of your employer's choice, remember, you are in control of you career. Take some time to regroup and assess what happen, then move on to bigger and better opportunities!

111

What will be asked in my employee exit interview?

Most companies will conduct an exit interview before you leave. You'll meet with your supervisor or someone from HR. The purpose of the interview is for the company to gain insights into why you are leaving. They can use this information to improve retention, adjust to company processes and policies, or to deal with any number of issues.

Since you are leaving, it is not in your best interest to bring up any unresolved issues or grievances. Be honest about your experience within the confines of things you've already officially communicated. Your goal is to ensure a positive relationship with the company upon your exit, even if you don't expect you'll ever work there again.

Your Job Search Toolkit

To support your full-time job search, you'll need several tools that represent you to your potential employer, including online platforms, documents, and techniques. A resume, a career roadmap, a LinkedIn profile, and a business card are all tools used in the standard job search. In addition, consider support apps for time tracking, project management, and scheduling.

112
How do I create a career roadmap?

Your career roadmap is a plan that helps you achieve your dream. Before beginning the steps of the search for a specific job, start with a long-term view by creating a career roadmap. Let's first define what a career roadmap is: a living document that identifies how to reach milestones in your career. You'll modify it as you progress throughout your career.

It's difficult for most—at any age—to imagine what you'll be doing in five, ten or even twenty years. But that is the goal of the career roadmap. Do you expect to be in one industry? Will you start in corporate and move to nonprofit? Will you work for a startup and then launch your own? You may have envisioned some broad ideas that can be further delineated.

Components of the career roadmap

Your career roadmap will indicate the key milestones, as best as you can imagine, that are required to reach your career goals. It could have three milestones, or ten, depending on how much you know about your goals. Ideally, you will map your milestones to a completion date, but you can also just create them as a loose guide. Milestones might include:

- **EDUCATION**—degree programs, certificates, continuing education, skills training, etc.
- **NETWORK**—connection with individuals you'd like to meet that could help support your career or provide insights, mentors you'd like to work with
- **ORGANIZATIONS**—joining and participating in organizations in your industry to build your network and learn more about your business

- **VOLUNTEERISM**—volunteering for causes you feel passionately about, gaining experience by contributing your expertise
- **ROLES**—deciding on a job, speaking with others who have that job title, landing the right job
- **COMPANIES**—identifying your favorite companies, researching those companies, meeting people from your top company, working for one of your favorite companies
- **ACCOMPLISHMENTS**—building an app, leading a national advertising campaign, leading a team of fifty people, etc.
- **ACTIVITIES**—playing sports to build strength and confidence, acting to discover and express emotions or your creative expression
- **NOTORIETY**—winning awards, honorary degrees, or press

Let's hear what Kevin says about creating a career roadmap:

Planning should be fun!

Planning your career should be a fun experience. It marks the beginning of a new journey that ideally aligns your interests with your talents to achieve goals you've set for your life.

Defining your career path doesn't need to be an overwhelming process where you plan your entire career. Chances are the job you're in now or the next one you take on will not be your last. Your approach to your career path should prepare you for change and allow you to make the best career decision at critical moments in your life.

Start with a bias towards action. Focus on what's most important right now, and define your goals. Once your goals are clear, relentlessly pursue them and leverage every resource available to you. Understanding your short and long-term goals and aligning them with your talents and resources will save you time and allow you to make better career decisions.

Understanding what's most important to you

What's important to you right now that's pushing you to make a change? Maybe you're just entering the job market, seeking greater financial security or looking to improve your balance of time.

Start by setting some easy goals that allow you to explore opportunities. You can always change your goals, so there's no risk in exploring. Follow all leads until you can make an informed decision if the opportunity is right or not. This journey may provide you with new ideas and opportunities you never even knew existed.

Years ago, in his early twenties, my friend was invited to a swing dance class in Los Angeles, California. He had always loved music and enjoyed dancing, but had never taken a lesson. At the end of the class, the instructor and owner of the studio asked him if he'd like to learn to be an instructor. My friend was a natural. Over the next twelve years he danced competitively around the world, he won international awards, built a chain of dance studios and became the lead choreographer and a performer for one of the largest dance programs on a major television network.

My friend had a gift and had the fortune of having someone else see his talent and offer him an opportunity. If he had been asked to list his long-term career goals at the time he would have struggled. He knew he loved music and dancing, and he followed opportunity after opportunity and worked hard every step of the way. He was fearless and his interests and talents aligned with opportunity at the perfect time.

Based on my experience, most people are not as lucky as my friend. Many struggle with transforming their career reality into their dream job. Some struggle with balancing career goals with other life priorities, while others don't set goals at all and passionately follow ideas only to fall short of achieving their dreams.

Keeping your career plan simple and focused on what you can do right now and exploring all opportunities will improve your success in achieving your goals. Start by defining a few short-term goals you think you can achieve in the next few months and one or two larger goals you can achieve in the next 12-24 months. Remember to keep your longer-term career goals in mind to ensure you're still heading in the right direction.

Not everyone is born with innate dancing talent and exceeds their career dream early in life. The formula of aligning your goals with your talents and exploring all opportunities is a great strategy to help you find your career path.[193]

113

What is a pitch, and how do I create one?

When you network—really, when you meet anyone—you need a pitch. What's a pitch? It's a succinct, branded, and memorable summary of you as a potential employee. It can be evolved from your mission statement. The reaction you want to elicit after delivering your pitch is, "Wow, impressive. I'd like to know more about you!"

Create both a short pitch and a long pitch. Your short pitch is one sentence that summarizes—in a clear and engaging way—what you do, how you do it, and for whom. If you are in a room full of other people with the same skills and experience, your pitch should be the most memorable.

Your long pitch should be about twenty seconds and should explain the short pitch in more detail. Think of it as the mini story of you, with a beginning, middle, and end. For your professional life, define what you've done, what you're doing, and what you plan on doing next, all with an engaging style.

Write both pitches down, and memorize them. Then, record yourself reciting both pitches. Know them by heart so they roll off your tongue. The long pitch should end with an ask, or "call to action," that is relevant to the situation—a follow-up call, sending a resume, connecting on LinkedIn, exchanging business cards, etc. If the pitch is the start of the dialogue, leave the ask for the end of the conversation.

Short pitch example

Hi, I'm Lavern Masters. I'm a Social Media Marketer working with entertainment clients to create fun and engaging campaigns that go viral.

Long pitch example

> Hi, I'm Lavern Masters. I'm a Social Media Marketer working with entertainment business clients to create fun and engaging campaigns that go viral. During my summer internship for Famous Actor, my Facebook campaign contributed to a 200% increase in shares in just one week. When I graduate in the fall, my goal is to work for a major Hollywood studio on their social media team, developing the strategy and creating content for national campaigns. Could we stay in touch on LinkedIn?

Let's compare that to a short and long pitch that are not thought out.

Short pitch example

> Hi, I'm Lavern. I want to work in Social Media.

Long pitch example

> Hi, I'm Lavern. I want to work in Social Media. I'd like to work for a big film company in their Social Media department. Do you know of any jobs?

Which pitch would make you happy to help that person? Spreading your excitement about your work makes you memorable.

114
What makes a resume great?

Your resume is a summary of your work experience, education, and goals. It is a marketing document that influences a potential employer's first impression of you. Parameters for what makes a resume great fluctuate along with other job searching trends. Be sure to pay attention to the current trends, but don't forget to make your personal brand shine through. Remember that the average time spent reading your resume will be six seconds.[194]

Best practices of resume writing (that don't change):

- To start, make sure your resume aligns with the job description of the position for which you're applying. If you have the desired skills, they should be in your resume!
- Put your contact info at the top.
- Include a bulleted table of skills (below contact info and title) to highlight your skills.
- The length will depend on your work experience.
- Utilize metrics and key words.
- Minimize educational info.
- Use a standard format.

To summarize, expert Charlotte Lee brings it down to basics and suggests the use of:

- White space
- Impactful words
- Metrics[195]

Consider working with a company that professionally writes resumes or a career coach. It is an important document, and it can be difficult to perceive the best in yourself. An expert will also be aware of trends in the marketplace.

115
What should I write in my cover letter?

A cover letter serves as a personal introduction to your prospective employer and accompanies your resume when applying for a job. It's your opportunity to stand out from the crowd, point out your unique understanding of the company and express how you're the right person for the role.

Consider integrating some of the information you've already researched about the company, the executive leadership, and current industry issues, or something you found out about the role from glassdoor.com or other employees.

Although your cover letter should be custom crafted for each application, you can create a template and modify it. Mirror the "voice" of the company. If it is a casual startup, write with a friendly tone. If it is an established financial institution, your style should be formal. Follow the standard business letter format (see example which follows). The body content should include:

1 **WHY YOU WANT THE JOB**—Talk about your personal connection to the company and your enthusiasm for the role.

2 **WHY YOU ARE THE RIGHT PERSON FOR THE JOB**—Define a few key skills and experiences that make you the right fit.

3 **SHOW YOUR UNDERSTANDING OF THE COMPANY**—Note a challenge they're experiencing that you could solve, or mention some other point that indicates you know the company.

4 **NAME ANY REFERENCES**—Let the hiring manager know that you already have connections in the company.

Per career counseling expert Charlotte Lee, it should be:

- "Three paragraphs only"
- "Contain a 'hook'"
- "End with a call to action"[196]

Usually, when applying online, the system will not allow the submission of a cover letter. As a work around, you could include the cover letter in the same document as your resume. If you have the hiring manager's contact info, follow up with an email to ensure they received your application.

116

What should I write in my thank you letter?

After every interview, send a thank you email to the interviewer. "According to a survey by online job-matching service The Ladders, 75 percent of interviewers said that receiving a thank-you letter from a candidate affects their decision-making process."[197] In addition to being a common courtesy, a thank you letter influences how you will be remembered by the interviewer.

The contents of the email should be short, highlighting key takeaways you'd like the interviewer to remember. If there were shared interests or other commonalities during the interview, mention one. If, on reflection, you'd answer a question differently, use this opportunity to recast your response. Be sure to clearly state your thanks, and affirm that you are enthusiastic about the job.

Double check all grammar and spelling, and ensure you have the correct spelling for the name and email address of the interviewer.

Don't expect to get a response right away. In fact, you may not receive a response. HR departments sometimes request there be no correspondence between hiring managers and candidates to prevent the communication of unsanctioned information. However, feel free to contact the hiring manager to request a status update if you haven't heard anything in a week.

Per our expert, Charlotte Lee, the main goal of the thank you letter is to "make someone feel great when receiving it."[198]

Template for thank you email after job is offered

Dear [HR Associate, Hiring Manager]:

After our phone call today, I wanted to thank you for the job offer of [Job Title] at [Company Name]. I am very excited to hear this great news!

I will look for the official offer in my [email or mail] no later than [date]. Once I have the chance to review the details, I will provide you with my decision by [date].

Please contact me if you need anything else.

Again, thank you for this opportunity.

Sincerely,
[Your Name]
[email address]
[phone number]
[mailing address]

Template for accepting job offer

Dear [HR Associate, Hiring Manager]:

I am very excited to formally announce my acceptance of the offer of [Job Title] at [Company Name]. I will submit all required documents by [date].

Working for [Company Name] is an honor, and I look forward to contributing to the success of my team and the company.

Please contact me if you need anything else.

Thank you for this opportunity and all your support in this process.

Sincerely,
    [Your Name]
    [email address]
    [phone number]
    [mailing address]

Template for job offer rejection

Dear [HR Associate, Hiring Manager]:

As per our phone call today, I wanted to follow up on the job offer of [Job Title] at [Company Name].

While I appreciate the offer, after careful consideration, I am withdrawing my candidacy to pursue another offer that more closely aligns with my career plans.

I thank you and the team for your time and your offer. If it okay with you, I would like to keep in touch in hopes that we may have another opportunity to work together.

Sincerely,
[Your Name]
[email address]
[phone number]
[mailing address]

117
How do I build a great portfolio?

If you are in a field that produces creative output—design or writing, for example—provide samples of your work in addition to your resume. Present this portfolio of work on your own website (be sure to keep a backup) or on another online platform.

Be clear about your audience. Who is hiring you? What examples do they want to see? Organize your work with a coherent structure and naming scheme. For example, categorize your work by industry or project type—all work for financial services companies together or all logos together. Name your files using a descriptive system: companyname_ abbreviatedprojecttype_date. Enhance the visuals with the narratives behind the designs. The stories should include the project goal, success metrics, and the key tasks you executed.

If you have not created work professionally, meaning work that was paid for, include your best samples from internships or volunteer work. Professionals are not interested in school work. To bolster your professional portfolio, ask for commissions from friends and family who are in business. Offer your work at a discounted rate to generate a good volume. You'll also get great experience by working with real clients.

118

What are best practices for using LinkedIn?

LinkedIn is an online platform for professionals in most every industry. Statistics compiled by Craig Smith show the depth and breadth of LinkedIn's reach: 500 million users and 128 million users in the U.S. (meaning 70% are from outside of the U.S.). His research also found that profiles with professional headshots get 14% more views, and listing at least five skills on your profile increases profile views by 17 times.[199]

As the industry standard professional platform, LinkedIn is used for four key activities: managing your professional network, searching for a job, keeping up with professional news and information, and publishing content to demonstrate your expertise. (LinkedIn has good tutorials, and there are several articles that can show the details of how to access these features.)

Your first move is to create your profile.

Creating and sharing your profile

At a minimum, create a profile on LinkedIn, and keep it current. The profile is composed of the following sections:

1 **PROFILE PHOTO**—Post a professional headshot if possible. If not, have a friend take a photo of you dressed in business attire appropriate for your field.

2 **NAME, TITLE, COMPANY**—Just that. Straightforward, right? However, consider how to include keywords in your job title.

3 **BRAND SUMMARY**—Modify this from your resume, and include keywords that someone would use when searching for professionals with your expertise.

4 **[WORK] EXPERIENCE**—List your last 3-5 jobs or internships.

5 **EDUCATION**—List your university degrees and any other credentialed learning. Graduation date is not required.

6 **VOLUNTEER EXPERIENCE**—List volunteer experiences that show your values and skills as they relate to your job title.

7 **FEATURED SKILLS AND ENDORSEMENTS**—Add skills—in the form of keyword phrases—in a prioritized order, with those most relevant to the job you seek at the top. Manage your skills by adding, deleting, and reordering your skills list. In addition, your first-degree connections can endorse you for skills and vice versa. You have the option of deleting any of the endorsers for any skill on your list. Endorsers who share the same skill are more highly valued in validating your skill.

8 **RECOMMENDATIONS**—Get at least one senior person and one peer from each job to recommend you on LinkedIn. It's best to ask while you still work there, and always reciprocate the recommendation. Some people are not comfortable providing recommendations, so don't be offended if you get turned down. There is a feature where you can send a reminder if someone doesn't respond to your request right away.

9 **ACCOMPLISHMENTS**—This includes certifications, courses, honors and awards, languages, patents, projects, publications, test scores, and organizations.

10 **INTERESTS**—List all the groups to which you belong. Consider how your interests reflect your professional brand. If you work in a conservative industry, don't list political activism as an interest.

As you write your profile, keep these points in mind:

- There is debate as to whether it's better to write in the first person or third person. Third person is preferable because reading a profile with a lot of "I's" is not as interesting. First person sounds more "personable," but your primary goal is to sound professional.

- Pull content from your resume, but you can be less formal and express your accomplishments and attributes with more of a marketing spin.
- Describe 3-5 key accomplishments, and include metrics to show your success (e.g. drove $1 million in sales per year in X, increased revenue by doing X). Define key character attributes that were relevant to your accomplishment (e.g. strong leader, quick decision maker, negotiator, innovator).

If you find writing the profile challenging, here are three tricks to spark your imagination.

1 Build a timeline of your achievements at your current job. From there, you can extract key points.
2 Record yourself talking about your accomplishments on the job using a text to speech app. Edit for key points.
3 Review your competitors' profiles (people with the same job title in similar companies) for inspiration.

Customize the URL for your profile, and include it in your email signature. The original URL provided automatically by LinkedIn will not be memorable. Edit to best reflect your name. (I was an early adopter so mine is linkedin.com/in/marya.)

Managing your professional network

Everyone you meet along your career path has the potential to offer a job opportunity, introduce you to new connections, or share valuable information. To stay in touch, use LinkedIn as an expanded address book. Who you keep in your address book is up to you. You can choose to only accept requests from people you know or have directly met, or you can accept anyone who requests a connection with you.

More first level connections translate into better ranking for searches on your job title, so there is value to accepting everyone. However, the advantage of only connecting to people you know, is you'll have a better relationship with your network. You can confidently recommend and introduce people and ask for support when you need it.

If you are just starting on LinkedIn, import your existing address book. Then, add people you know who are not in your address book, but are on LinkedIn. Find contacts from a direct search (although that may be time consuming), or explore existing groups that might include people you know. You usually must join a group before seeing the other members, but the titles will give you clues. Groups are organized by job titles, areas of focus, company alumni, university alumni, and other types of connection.

After searching for a person, you can invite them to connect. Be sure to add a personalized note instead of sending a "blind" request. You can do this by going to their profile and clicking on the ellipsis (...) and selecting "Personalize Invite" from the drop down menu. (Note that the process may change as LinkedIn updates its user interface.) In the note, remind them of how you know them, or if you don't, why your connection would be valuable. Continue to grow your LinkedIn network by adding people you meet at networking events, on the job and through other connections.

Gathering news and information

On your newsfeed, you'll see posts from your network and companies you've "liked." (Ads are also included now.)

To get information and make new connections, you can join groups. There is a group for every professional category imaginable. In groups, you can post and have conversations with members. Focus on active groups with relevant topics where you can get specific question answered or share your expertise. Is it worth your time? Evaluate that for yourself. Stick to the rule of time-effectiveness: the time you invest should at least equal your return.

Publishing professional content

For your LinkedIn posts, consider what content will present you as an expert in your industry, a thought leader. It's fine to repost and comment on other content occasionally, but it's best to create original content. Post on your own blog first, then link to it on LinkedIn, or post work samples in the portfolio or slideshare formats.

Interacting with your network

1   **RECOMMENDATIONS**—This function allows a colleague to post a recommendation for you. You request a recommendation by defining your relationship and role, then sending a short customizable request. Provide some direction for how you want to express your brand. It is common courtesy to offer a recommendation in return.

2   **MESSAGING**—This sends a message to a first level contact that appears on LinkedIn, and sends an email notification (if turned on) to the recipient. You can respond directly to a LinkedIn message from the email.

3   **NOTIFICATIONS**—LinkedIn's Notifications function alerts you when someone in your network experiences an event (birthday, promotion, new job, etc.). It's a great way to stay in touch.

119

How can I best curate social media channels?

There are many social media channels, and you are one person managing your career, not a major business enterprise. Select the social media that will support your career progress best. If you are a writer or marketer, you should be active in the channels you expect to create content for or manage in your job, such as Twitter and/or Facebook. If you are a designer, or other visually-based artist, you may add Instagram or Pinterest for static media and YouTube or Vimeo for dynamic images.

Curate the one or two best channels to support your career advancement and professional brand. Research what social media others in your field predominantly use. LinkedIn should be used by most everyone.

Social media can be a valuable tool to help promote your business, or it can be a time sucker. Always consider your return on investment. For example, if you are spending an hour a day on it, and your hourly rate is $100, in one month that is $2,000 worth of your time. Did you get $2,000 of value back from your posts?

Remember, there are two major groups of marketing value: sales-driven marketing and brand-awareness marketing. That translates into job offers or recognition of your brand: requests for speaking engagements, contributor to an article or other press worthy opportunities.

Final Thoughts

What can you do to ensure you enjoy your career and have it deliver the success you expect? The best approach is to consider your career over time:

- **LEARN FROM YOUR PAST**—Increase your knowledge base by learning from both your failures and successes. Highlight completed milestones, and build on what you love.
- **ACHIEVE IN THE PRESENT**—Use the present to document accomplishments as they happen. Ensure they are telling the story you need to tell.
- **ENVISION THE FUTURE**—Challenge yourself to the be the best you! Plan your next move.

120

What are the 7 Rs for cultivating your career?

Please keep these 7 Rs in mind as you progress through your career.

- **REWARDING**—Don't just search for a job; strategically build a career that is rewarding to you and gives back to others. Aspire to be your best.
- **RELISH**—Life is short. Do what it takes to be grateful and enjoy each moment.
- **RESPONSIBLE**—You are the master of your career. Own it and take care of it. Acknowledge the wins and the losses.
- **REFLECT**—Take time to pause, shutdown. Sense your limitations and your potential. Invest time to nourish your mind, body, spirit, and career for a lifetime.
- **RESILIENT**—It's okay to fail, to be afraid, to not know what you want. Be patient with yourself as you get back on track after rough patches (we all have them).
- **RELATIONSHIPS**—Your success depends on the strength of your network and the relationships you build. Be authentic with people and your behavior will usually be returned.
- **RESEARCH**—Landing the best jobs is tough. Use all the information you can access, and form a strategy for getting hired.

Thank you for taking this journey with me. I hope that you've found the answers you were looking for or have found a topic of interest for further research. As you see fit, share the knowledge you gained to help a friend. Best wishes in finding the X in your Career!

Bibliography

1   Duckworth, Angela. Grit. Vermilion, 2017.
2   The Merriam-Webster dictionary. Merriam-Webster, Incorporated, 2016.
3   IBID.
4   Gapper, John. "New 'Gig' Economy Spells End to Lifetime Careers." Financial Times, Financial Times, 5 Aug. 2015, www.ft.com/content/ab492ffc-3522-11e5-b05b-b01debd57852.
5   "12 Celebrities Who Were Discovered Out of the Blue." Fox News, FOX News Network, www.foxnews.com/entertainment/slideshow/2013/05/14/12-celebrities-who-were-discovered-out-blue.html#/slide/11.
6   The Merriam-Webster dictionary. Merriam-Webster, Incorporated, 2016.
7   Lawler, Annie. Personal interview. 13 Apr. 2017.
8   "Average Published Undergraduate Charges by Sector and by Carnegie Classification, 2017-18." Trends in Higher Education, trends.collegeboard.org/college-pricing/figures-tables/average-published-undergraduate-charges-sector-2016-17.
9   "The State of American Jobs." Pew Research Center's Social & Demographic Trends Project, 6 Oct. 2016, www.pewsocialtrends.org/2016/10/06/the-state-of-american-jobs/. p. 75
10 IBID, p. 16
11 IBID, p. 23
12 IBID, p. 80
13 Stuart, Nancy. Personal interview. 27 Feb. 2017.
14 Davidson, Adam. "Is College Tuition Really Too High?" The New York Times, The New York Times, 8 Sept. 2015, www.nytimes.com/2015/09/13/magazine/is-college-tuition-too-high.html.
15 IBID.
16 IBID.
17 IBID.
18 IBID.
19 IBID.

20 Cilluffo, Anthony. "5 facts about student loans." Pew Research Center,
    24 Aug, 2017,
    www.pewresearch.org/fact-tank/2017/08/24/5-facts-about-student-
    loans/.
21 IBID.
22 Staff, Marketplace. "Study: Millennials still struggling with student debt
    and underemployment." Marketplace, Marketplace,
    www.marketplace.org/2017/07/04/economy/study-millennials-still-
    struggling-student-debt-and-underemployment.
23 IBID.
24 IBID.
25 Kantrowitz, Mark. "Why Student Loan & Debt Crisis Is Worse Than
    People Think | Money." Time, Time, Jan. 11AD, 2016,
    time.com/money/4168510/why-student-loan-crisis-is-worse-than-
    people-think/.
26 "The State of American Jobs." Pew Research Center's Social &
    Demographic Trends Project, 6 Oct. 2016,
    www.pewsocialtrends.org/2016/10/06/the-state-of-american-jobs/.
27 "Rewriting the Rules for the Digital Age." Global Human Capital
    Trends Report,
    www2.deloitte.com/content/dam/Deloitte/global/Documents/
    HumanCapital/hc-2017-global-human-capital-trends-gx.pdf. p. 29
28 IBID, p. 30
29 Garrett, Rachel. Personal interview. 2 Mar. 2017.
30 Whitney, Will. Personal interview. 24 Feb. 2017.
31 Bresnick, Josh. Personal interview. 28 Sep. 2017.
32 Norris, Kevin. Personal interview. 7 Apr. 2017.
33 Schlader, Ted. Personal interview. 11 May 2017.
34 Bershaw, Alex. Personal interview. 25 Aug, 2017.
35 Marryat, Kathy. Personal interview. 27 May 2017.
36 Rybak, Cathy. Personal interview. 13 Aug. 2017.
37 Mayzing, Teena. Personal interview. 4 Dec. 2017.
38 "Absences." U.S. Bureau of Labor Statistics, U.S. Bureau of Labor
    Statistics,
    www.bls.gov/cps/lfcharacteristics.htm#contingent.
39 "Fact Sheet #13: Am I an Employee?: Employment Relationship Under
    the Fair Labor Standards Act (FLSA)." U.S. Department of Labor,
    www.dol.gov/whd/regs/compliance/whdfs13.pdf.
40 "Rewriting the Rules for the Digital Age." Global Human Capital
    Trends Report,
    www2.deloitte.com/content/dam/Deloitte/global/Documents/
    HumanCapital/hc-2017-global-human-capital-trends-gx.pdf. p. 128
41 Chamberlain, Andrew. "Looking Ahead: 5 Jobs Trends to Watch in 2017."
    Glassdoor Economic Research, Dec. 2016,
    www.glassdoor.com/research/studies/jobs-trends-2017/.

42 Schwartz, Jeff, et al. "The Gig Economy." DU Press, Deloitte Insights, 29 Feb. 2016, dupress.deloitte.com/dup-us-en/focus/human-capital-trends/2016/gig-economy-freelance-workforce.html.

43 "Rewriting the Rules for the Digital Age." Global Human Capital Trends Report, www2.deloitte.com/content/dam/Deloitte/global/Documents/HumanCapital/hc-2017-global-human-capital-trends-gx.pdf. p. 128

44 Duhigg, Charles. "How to Form Healthy Habits in Your 20s." The New York Times, The New York Times, 18 Oct. 2016, www.nytimes.com/2016/10/19/well/mind/how-to-form-healthy-habits-in-your-20s.html?_r=0.

45 Olson, Lindsay. "Sitting Disease: The Slow, Silent and Sedentary Killer of the American Workforce." U.S. News, 22 Aug. 2013, 10:09, money.usnews.com/money/blogs/outside-voices-careers/2013/08/22/are-you-suffering-from-sitting-disease.

46 Laskowski, M.D. Edward R. "How Much Exercise Do You Really Need?" Mayo Clinic, Mayo Foundation for Medical Education and Research, 20 Aug. 2016, www.mayoclinic.org/healthy-lifestyle/fitness/expert-answers/exercise/faq-20057916.

47 Duckworth, Angela. Grit. Vermilion, 2017.

48 Garrett, Rachel. Personal interview. 2 Mar. 2017.

49 The Merriam-Webster dictionary. Merriam-Webster, Incorporated, 2016.

50 Lawler, Annie. Personal interview. 13 Apr. 2017.

51 Dinsmore, Scott. "How to Find Work You Love." TED: Ideas Worth Spreading, Oct. 2012, www.ted.com/talks/scott_dinsmore_how_to_find_work_you_love.

52 Norris, Kevin. Personal interview. 9 Mar. 2017.

53 "MBTI Basics." The Myers & Briggs Foundation , www.myersbriggs.org/my-mbti-personality-type/mbti-basics/.

54 Olsen, Jesse E., and Peter Gahan. "Why using Myers-Briggs at work Might Be a Terrible Idea (MBTI)." The Conversation, 4 Sept. 2014, theconversation.com/why-using-myers-briggs-at-work-might-be-a-terrible-idea-mbti-31178.

55 Morse, Anita. Personal interview. 22 Mar. 2017.

56 IBID.

57 Insider, Business. "18 Successful People Who Get by on Very Little Sleep." Financial Post, 5 Oct. 2013, business.financialpost.com/business-insider/18-successful-people-who-get-by-on-very-little-sleep.

58 "Consequences of Insufficient Sleep." Healthy Sleep, Harvard Medical School, healthysleep.med.harvard.edu/healthy/matters/consequences.

59 Olson, Eric J. "How Many Hours of Sleep Do You Need?" Mayo Clinic, Mayo Foundation for Medical Education and Research, 6 Apr. 2016, www.mayoclinic.org/healthy-lifestyle/adult-health/expert-answers/ how-many-hours-of-sleep-are-enough/faq-20057898.

60 Colvin, Geoff. "Do Successful CEOs Sleep Less Than Everyone Else?" Fortune, 18 Nov. 2015, fortune.com/2015/11/18/sleep-habits-donald-trump/.

61 Bratman, Gregory N., et al. "Gregory N. Bratman." Proceedings of the National Academy of Sciences, National Acad Sciences, 28 May 2015, www.pnas.org/content/112/28/8567.abstract.

62 IBID.

63 Iliff, Jeff. "One more reason to get a good night's sleep." TED: Ideas worth spreading, Sept. 2014, www.ted.com/talks/jeff_iliff_one_more_reason_to_get_a_good_night_ s_sleep?referrer=playlist-how_does_my_brain_work.

64 Damasio, Antonio. "The quest to understand consciousness." TED: Ideas worth spreading, Mar. 2011, www.ted.com/talks/antonio_damasio_the_quest_to_understand_ consciousness/transcript?referrer=playlist-how_does_my_brain_work.

65 IBID.

66 Colman, Andrew M. A Dictionary of Psychology. 3rd ed., Oxford University Press, 2008.

67 Rubin, Gretchen. "Ta-Da! The Launch of My Quiz on the Four Tendencies. Learn About Yourself!" Gretchen Rubin, 14 Jan. 2015, gretchenrubin.com/happiness_project/2015/01/ta-da-the-launch-of- my-quiz-on-the-four-tendencies-learn-about-yourself/.

68 IBID.

69 Maslow, A. H. "A theory of human motivation." APA PsycNet, American Psychological Association, psycnet.apa.org/record/1943-03751-001.

70 Halvorson, Heidi Grant. "The Surprising Key to Finding the Right Job For You." Forbes, Forbes Magazine, 18 Apr. 2013, www.forbes.com/sites/heidigranthalvorson/2013/04/18/the-surprising- key-to-finding-the-right-job-for-you/#667669a94672.

71 IBID.

72 Story, Louise. "Anywhere the Eye Can See, It's Likely to See an Ad." The New York Times, The New York Times, 14 Jan. 2007, www.nytimes.com/2007/01/15/business/media/15everywhere.html.

73 Hinckley, David. "Average American Watches 5 Hours of TV per Day." NY Daily News, 5 Mar. 2014, www.nydailynews.com/life-style/average-american-watches- 5-hours-tv-day-article-1.1711954.

74 Perez, Sarah. "U.S. consumers now spend 5 hours per day on mobile devices." TechCrunch, TechCrunch, 3 Mar. 2017, techcrunch.com/2017/0 3/03/u-s-consumers-now-spend-5-hours-per-day-on-mobile-devices/.

75 Isidore, Chris, and Tami Luhby. "Turns out Americans Work Really Hard...but Some Want to Work Harder." CNNMoney, Cable News Network, 9 July 2015, 17:01, money.cnn.com/2015/07/09/news/economy/americans-work-bush/.

76 "Self-Assessment." Career Planning Service, 30 Oct. 2017, www.mcgill.ca/caps/students/explore/self-assessment.

77 Sandeen, Cathy. "The Emerging World of Alternative Credentials." Higher Education Today, American Council on Education, 1 Oct. 2013, www.higheredtoday.org/2013/10/01/the-emerging-world-of-alternative-credentials/.

78 Rüegger, Reto. "Hard Skills vs. Soft Skills: Are Soft Skills Winning?" The HR Tech Weekly®, 15 Nov. 2016, hrtechweekly.com/2016/11/15/hard-skills-vs-soft-skills-are-soft-skills-winning/.

79 IBID.

80 Beaton, Caroline. "Top Employers Say Millennials Need These 4 Skills in 2017." Forbes, Forbes Magazine, 9 Jan. 2017, www.forbes.com/sites/carolinebeaton/2017/01/06/top-employers-say-millennials-need-these-4-skills-in-2017/#3660a22a7fe4.

81 "Forty Percent of Employers Plan to Hire Full-Time, Permanent Employees in 2017, CareerBuilder's Annual Job Forecast Finds." Career Builder, 6 Jan. 2017, www.careerbuilder.com/share/aboutus/pressreleasesdetail.aspx?ed=12%2F31%2F2017&id=pr983&sd=1%2F6%2F2017.

82 "The State of American Jobs." Pew Research Center's Social & Demographic Trends Project, 6 Oct. 2016, www.pewsocialtrends.org/2016/10/06/the-state-of-american-jobs/.

83 IBID, p. 11

84 Starner, Tom. "So-Called 'Soft' Skills Remain Hard to Find." HR Dive, 31 Aug. 2016, www.hrdive.com/news/so-called-soft-skills-remain-hard-to-find/425423/.

85 Craig, Ryan. "Blame Bad Applicant Tracking for the Soft Skills Shortage at Your Company." TechCrunch, 5 Mar. 2017, techcrunch.com/2017/03/05/blame-bad-applicant-tracking-for-the-soft-skills-shortage-at-your-company/.

86 Hoppe, Michael H. Active Listening: Improve Your Ability to Listen and Lead. CCL Publications, 2006.

87 Shellenbarger, Sue. "Tuning In: Improving Your Listening Skills." The Wall Street Journal, Dow Jones & Company, 22 July 2014, www.wsj.com/articles/tuning-in-how-to-listen-better-1406070727.

88 Solomon, Susan. Personal interview. 21 Feb. 2017.

89 IBID.

90 Carey, Brian. "Networking: Boost Sales by Making the Right Connections." QuickBooks, Intuit, 24 Nov. 2016,

quickbooks.intuit.com/r/marketing/networking-boost-sales-by-making-the-right-connections/. Adam Small quotation

91 Haselhof, Luke. Personal interview. 6 Jun. 2017.

92 Bieger, Jeremy. Personal interview. 20 Feb. 2017.

93 McIntosh, Bob. "80% of today's jobs are landed through networking." RecruitingBlogs, 26 Mar. 2012, www.recruitingblogs.com/profiles/blogs/80-of-today-s-jobs-are-landed-through-networking.

94 Haseloff, Luke. Personal interview. 4 May 2017.

95 Yusupova, Nelly. Personal interview. 23 Mar. 2017.

96 IBID.

97 Bieger, Jeremy. Personal interview. 20 Feb. 2017.

98 The Merriam-Webster dictionary. Merriam-Webster, Incorporated, 2016.

99 Black, Holly. "Louise Nevelson: The Supreme Grandmother of Sculpture." AnOther, 9 Nov. 2016, www.anothermag.com/fashion-beauty/9240/louise-nevelson-the-supreme-grandmother-of-sculpture.

100 "The Future of Jobs: Employment, Skills, and Workforce Strategy for the Fourth Industrial Revolution." Global Challenge Insight Report, www3.weforum.org/docs/WEF_Future_of_Jobs.pdf. p. 3

101 Thompson, Derek. "A World Without Work." The Atlantic, Atlantic Media Company, 6 Nov. 2017, www.theatlantic.com/magazine/archive/2015/07/world-without-work/395294/.

102 Beckett, Andy. "Post-Work: the radical idea of a world without jobs." The Guardian, Guardian News and Media, 19 Jan. 2018, www.theguardian.com/news/2018/jan/19/post-work-the-radical-idea-of-a-world-without-jobs.

103 Fu, Lisa. "The Wealth Gap in the U.S. Is Worse Than In Russia or Iran." Fortune, 1 Aug. 2017, fortune.com/2017/08/01/wealth-gap-america/.

104 "Country Comparison: Distribution of Family Income - GINI Index." Central Intelligence Agency, Central Intelligence Agency, www.cia.gov/library/publications/resources/the-world-factbook/rankorder/2172rank.html.

105 "An Investment Manager's View on the Top 1%." Power in America, Who Rules America?, Jan. 2012, www2.ucsc.edu/whorulesamerica/power/investment_manager.html.

106 IBID.

107 Evans, John. "What Impact Is Climate Change Having on Jobs?" World Economic Forum, 8 Dec. 2015, www.weforum.org/agenda/2015/12/what-impact-is-climate-change-having-on-jobs/.

108 IBID.

109 "The Gig Economy Study." Workplace Trends, 3 May 2016, workplacetrends.com/the-gig-economy-study/.

110 "Rewriting the Rules for the Digital Age." Global Human Capital Trends Report, www2.deloitte.com/content/dam/Deloitte/global/Documents/ HumanCapital/hc-2017-global-human-capital-trends-gx.pdf. p. 9

111 "A Future That Works: Automation, Employment, and Productivity." McKinsey&Company, docs.wixstatic.com/ugd/ 2ec1b9_2ec98a14ada843ed9bd6d1e2c7b4daaf.pdf. p. 1

112 Drum, Kevin. "You Will Lose Your Job to a Robot-and Sooner than You Think." Mother Jones, 31 Oct. 2017, www.motherjones.com/politics/2017/10/you-will-lose-your-job-to-a-robot-and-sooner-than-you-think/.

113 IBID.

114 IBID.

115 White, Martha. "Here's How Long It Really Takes to Get a Job | Money." Time, Time, 22 Oct. 2015, time.com/money/4053899/how-long-it-takes-to-get-hired/.

116 "Pay Equity & Discrimination." Employment, Education, & Economic Change, Institute for Women's Policy Research, iwpr.org/issue/employment-education-economic-change/pay-equity-discrimination/#sthash.3G5NXzdf.dpuf.

117 "Women in Male-Dominated Industries and Occupations." Catalyst, 30 May 2017, www.catalyst.org/knowledge/women-male-dominated-industries-and-occupations.

118 IBID.

119 "Employed and unemployed full- and part-Time workers by age, sex, race, and Hispanic or Latino ethnicity." U.S. Bureau of Labor Statistics, U.S. Bureau of Labor Statistics, 8 Feb. 2017, www.bls.gov/cps/cpsaat08.htm.

120 Rashid, Brian. "The Rise Of The Freelancer Economy." Forbes, Forbes Magazine, 26 Jan. 2016, www.forbes.com/sites/brianrashid/2016/01/26/the-rise-of-the-freelancer-economy/#40b178b4379a.

121 "PINC-01. Selected Characteristics of People 15 Years and Over, by Total Money Income, Work Experience, Race, Hispanic Origin, and Sex." U.S. Census Bureau, www.census.gov/data/tables/time-series/demo/income-poverty/ cps-pinc/pinc-01.html.

122 IBID.

123 Smith, Jacquelyn. "The 30 highest-Paying jobs in America." Business Insider, Business Insider, 23 Sept. 2015,

uk.businessinsider.com/top-paying-jobs-in-america-2015-9?r=US&IR=T
%2F#30-physicists-1.

124 Dill, Kathryn. "The 10 Best-Paying Jobs In America - pg.1." Forbes,
Forbes Magazine, 7 June 2016,
www.forbes.com/pictures/fjle45edjjh/
the-10-best-paying-jobs/#2c8f038c3368.

125 "Fastest Growing Occupations : Occupational Outlook Handbook:" U.S.
Bureau of Labor Statistics, U.S. Bureau of Labor Statistics, 24 Oct. 2017,
www.bls.gov/ooh/fastest-growing.htm.

126 Onink, Troy. "College Costs Could Total As Much As $334,000 In Four
Years." Forbes, Forbes Magazine, 31 Jan. 2015,
www.forbes.com/sites/troyonink/2015/01/31/college-could-cost-
as-much-as-334000-total-in-four-years/#29a77b3679ff.

127 IBID.

128 "8 College Degrees That Will Earn Your Money Back." Salary.com,
salary.com/8-college-degrees-that-will-earn-your-money-back/.

129 "8 College Degrees with the Worst Return on Investment." Salary.com,
salary.com/8-college-degrees-with-the-worst-return-on-investment/.

130 "Unemployment Rates for Metropolitan Areas." U.S. Bureau of Labor
Statistics, U.S. Bureau of Labor Statistics, 30 Nov. 2017,
www.bls.gov/web/metro/laummtrk.htm.

131 "Unemployment Rates for Metropolitan Areas." U.S. Bureau of Labor
Statistics, U.S. Bureau of Labor Statistics, 30 Nov. 2017,
www.bls.gov/web/metro/laummtrk.htm.

132 Bernardo, Richie. "2017's Best & Worst Cities for Jobs." WalletHub,
4 Jan. 2017,
wallethub.com/edu/best-cities-for-jobs/2173/.

133 IBID.

134 Strauss, Karsten. "U.S. Cities With The Fastest-Growing Economies."
Forbes, Forbes Magazine, 1 Dec. 2016,
www.forbes.com/sites/karstenstrauss/2016/12/01/u-s-cities-with-the-
fastest-growing-economies/#440d8a0c60ab.

135 "Industries with the fastest growing and most rapidly declining wage
and salary employment." U.S. Bureau of Labor Statistics, U.S. Bureau of
Labor Statistics, 24 Oct. 2017,
www.bls.gov/emp/ep_table_203.htm.

136 IBID.

137 "Frequently Asked Questions." Advocacy: the Voice of Small Business in
Government,
www.sba.gov/sites/default/files/FAQ_Sept_2012.pdf.

138 DeSilver, Drew. "10 Facts about American Workers." Pew Research
Center, 1 Sept. 2016,
www.pewresearch.org/fact-tank/2016/09/01/8-facts-
about-american-workers/.

139 "8 College Degrees with the Worst Return on Investment." Salary.com, salary.com/8-college-degrees-with-the-worst-return-on-investment/.

140 "North American Industry Classification System (NAICS) Main Page." (NAICS) Main Page, U.S. Census Bureau, 15 May 2012, www.census.gov/eos/www/naics/.

141 Day, Colin. "The Real Cost Of A Poor Hire." Forbes, Forbes Magazine, 16 May 2016, 4:06, www.forbes.com/sites/icims/2016/05/16/ the-real-cost-of-a-poor-hire/#28a9b209242f.

142 Bersin by Deloitte Research: US HR Organizations Spending Increases, Following a Rise in Employee Turnover. Cision: PRNewswire, 14 Jan. 2015, www.prnewswire.com/news-releases/bersin-by-deloitte-research-us-hr-organizations-spending-increases-following-a-rise-in-employee-turnover-300020651.html.

143 "About Us." Glassdoor, www.glassdoor.co.uk/about/index_input.htm.

144 Stuart, Nancy. Personal interview. 27 Feb. 2017.

145 Goudreau, Jenna. "The Best Jobs That Don't Require A Bachelor's Degree." Forbes, Forbes Magazine, 28 July 2012, www.forbes.com/sites/jennagoudreau/2012/06/21/the-best-jobs-that-dont-require-a-bachelors-degree/#e7d27d177a94.

146 "College Enrollment and Work Activity of 2016 High School Graduates." U.S. Bureau of Labor Statistics, U.S. Bureau of Labor Statistics, 27 Apr. 2017, www.bls.gov/news.release/hsgec.nr0.htm.

147 Anderberg, Jeremy. "Is College for Everyone? An Introduction and Timeline of College in America." The Art of Manliness, 28 Nov. 2017, www.artofmanliness.com/2014/03/05/is-college-for-everyone-an-introduction-and-timeline-of-college-in-america/.

148 Ryan, Camille L., and Kurt Bauman. Educational Attainment in the United States: 2015. U.S. Census Bureau, Mar. 2016, www.census.gov/content/dam/Census/library/publications/2016/demo/p20-578.pdf.

149 IBID.

150 Goudreau, Jenna. "The Best Jobs That Don't Require A Bachelor's Degree." Forbes, Forbes Magazine, 21 June 2012, 11:37, www.forbes.com/sites/jennagoudreau/2012/06/21/the-best-jobs-that-dont-require-a-bachelors-degree/#e7d27d177a94.

151 Logan, Julie. "Analysis of the Incidence of Dyslexia in Entrepreneurs and Its Implications." Cass Business School, citeseerx.ist.psu.edu/viewdoc/download?doi=10.1.1.385.7837&rep=rep1&type=pdf.

152 Martin, Emmie. "The 20 Best High-Paying Jobs in America for 2016."
Careers, Business Insider, 2 Feb. 2016, 9:00,
www.businessinsider.com/highest-paying-jobs-in-
america-for-2016-2016-1/#20-optometrist-1.

153 Dwyer, Christopher J. "The State of Contingent Workforce Management
2015-2016." Ardent Partners, Oct. 2015,
resources.fieldglass.com/rs/655-SDM-567/images/Ardent_Partners_The_
State_of_CWM_2015_Fieldglass.pdf?mkt_tok=3RkMMJWWfF9
wsRoivKzLZKXonjHpfsX67%2BQqWq%2B1lMI/0ER3fOvrPUfGjI4
ES8RnI%2BSLDwEYGJlv6SgFTLXAMbNk17gIXRY%3D.

154 Schwartz, Cindy. Personal interview. 20 Feb. 2017.

155 White, Martha C. "Here's How Long It Really Takes to Get a Job |
Money." Time, Time, 22 Oct. 2015,
time.com/money/4053899/how-long-it-takes-to-get-hired/.

156 "Should You Apply To A Job If You Don't Meet All The Requirements?"
Forbes, Forbes Magazine, 31 Mar. 2016,
www.forbes.com/sites/forbescoachescouncil/2016/03/31/should-you-
apply-to-that-job-if-you-dont-meet-all-the-requirements/#20e80326cb2d.

157 Google Careers, Google, careers.google.com/.

158 Morgan, Hannah. "Here's How Recruiters Really Fill Jobs." US News,
23 Sept. 2015, 10:47,
money.usnews.com/money/blogs/outside-voices-careers/2015/09/23/
heres-how-recruiters-really-fill-jobs.

159 Rapp, Kelin. Personal interview. 19 Feb. 2017.

160 Clennett, Ross. "Global Staffing Industry Sales Top $400 Billion."
Recruiting Blogs, 16 Oct. 2014, 7:49,
www.recruitingblogs.com/profiles/blogs/global-staffing-industry-
sales-top-400-billion.

161 Augustine, Amanda. "9 Questions to Ask During an Informational
Interview (And 1 to Avoid)." Ladders | Business News & Career Advice,
30 Sept. 2014,
www.theladders.com/career-advice/ask-these-questions-at-your-
next-informational-interview/.

162 Haseloff, Luke. Personal interview. 6 Jun. 2017.

163 Steinfeld, Trudy. "Decoding The Job Search: How To Beat The ATS
(Applicant Tracking System)." Forbes, Forbes Magazine, 31 May 2016,
www.forbes.com/sites/trudysteinfeld/2016/05/31/decoding-the-job-
search-how-to-beat-the-ats-applicant-tracking-system/#750b28856d84.

164 Lustman, Lewis. "The Truth About Applicant Tracking Systems (ATS) -
HireRight." Go to HireRight, 6 Mar. 2017,
www.hireright.com/blog/2017/03/the-truth-about-applicant-
tracking-systems-ats/.

165 Reid, Julie. Personal interview. 26 Mar. 2017.

166 Needleman, Sarah E. "Lifting the Curtain on the Hiring Process." The Wall Street Journal, Dow Jones & Company, 26 Jan. 2010, www.wsj.com/articles/ SB10001424052748703808904575025250789355156.

167 Reid, Julie. Personal interview. 26 Mar. 2017.

168 Howden, Daniel. "What is average interview to hire ratio? Recruiting KPIs that matter | Workable." Recruiting Resources: How to Recruit and Hire Better, 10 Oct. 2017, resources.workable.com/blog/interviews-per-hire-recruiting-metrics.

169 Hubben, Anne. Personal interview. 7 Mar. 2017.

170 Doyle, Alison. "Best Answers for the Top 10 Interview Questions." The Balance, 5 Nov. 2017, www.thebalance.com/top-interview-questions-and-best-answers-2061225.

171 Avenue, Next. "10 Job Interview Questions You Should Ask." Forbes, Forbes Magazine, 29 Nov. 2017, www.forbes.com/sites/nextavenue/2014/06/18/10-job-interview-questions-you-should-ask/#1f54382a191e.

172 Giang, Vivian. "9 Common Interview Questions That Are Actually Illegal." Business Insider, Business Insider, 21 Mar. 2012, www.businessinsider.com/9-illegal-interview-questions-that-sound-legal-2012-3.

173 IBID.

174 Hubben, Anne. Personal interview. 7 Mar. 2017.

175 Church, Michael O. "Discussion Board: How Often Are Job Offers Rescinded?" Quora, 28 Nov. 2012, www.quora.com/How-often-are-job-offers-rescinded.

176 Schwartz, Cindy. Personal interview. 20 Feb. 2017.

177 IBID.

178 Gaffney, Steven. Just be honest: authentic communication strategies that get results and last a lifetime. JMG Publishing, 2004.

179 Harter, Jim, and Amy Adkins. "Employees Want a Lot More From Their Managers." Gallup Inc., 8 Apr. 2015, news.gallup.com/businessjournal/182321/employees-lot-managers.aspx.

180 Capelli, Peter, and Anna Tavis. "The Future of Performance Reviews." Harvard Business Review, Oct. 2016, hbr.org/2016/10/the-performance-management-revolution.

181 IBID.

182 The Merriam-Webster Dictionary. Merriam-Webster, Incorporated, 2016.

183 Ericsson, K. Anders, and Robert Pool. Peak: Secrets from the New Science of Expertise. Mariner Books/Houghton Mifflin Harcourt, 2017.

184 Outsider, The Chief. "Most Leaders are Made Not Born-And They Need to be Developed." Chief Outsiders: Unique Among Strategic Marketing Consulting Firms, 24 Sept. 2014,

www.chiefoutsiders.com/blog/bid/98579/born-leader-or-made-leader-which-one-are-you.

185 Murphy, Bill. "How Humans of New York Went Viral on Facebook." Inc. com, Inc., 10 July 2013, www.inc.com/bill-murphy-jr/how-humans-of-new-york-got-nearly-1-million-facebook-likes.html.

186 "How Many Roman Catholics Are There in the World?" BBC News, BBC, 14 Mar. 2013, www.bbc.com/news/world-21443313.

187 Olmstead, Maegan. "Title IX and the Rise of Female Athletes in America." Women's Sports Foundation, 19 Oct. 2016, www.womenssportsfoundation.org/education/title-ix-and-the-rise-of-female-athletes-in-america/.

188 Emerson. "The bravest women in the world." Amnesty International, 5 Mar. 2015, www.amnesty.org.uk/blogs/campaigns/bravest-women-world.

189 Mehl, Ann. Personal interview. 31 Jul. 2017.

190 "Number of Jobs, Labor Market Experience, and Earnings Growth Among Americans at 50: Results from a Longitudinal Survey." Bureau of Labor Statistics, www.bls.gov/news.release/pdf/nlsoy.pdf.

191 Meister, Jeanne. "The Future of Work: Job Hopping Is the 'New Normal' for Millennials." Forbes, Forbes Magazine, 3 Jan. 2017, www.forbes.com/sites/jeannemeister/2012/08/14/the-future-of-work-job-hopping-is-the-new-normal-for-millennials/#6aaf9ab513b8.

192 Rapp, Kelin. Personal interview. 19 Feb. 2017.

193 Norris, Kevin. Personal interview. 7 Apr. 2017.

194 Evans, Will. "You Have 6 Seconds to Make an Impression: How Recruiters See Your Resume." Ladders, 12 Mar. 2012, www.theladders.com/career-advice/you-only-get-6-seconds-of-fame-make-it-count/.

195 Lee, Charlotte. Personal interview. 20 Feb 2017.

196 IBID.

197 Fallon, Nicole. "After the Interview: Sample Thank You Letters." Business News Daily, 20 Jan. 2017, www.businessnewsdaily.com/5578-sample-thank-you-letters.html.

198 Lee, Charlotte. Personal interview. 20 Feb 2017.

199 Smith, Craig. "220 Amazing LinkedIn Statistics and Facts." DMR, 21 Nov. 2017, expandedramblings.com/index.php/by-the-numbers-a-few-important-linkedin-stats/.

About the Author

 Marya's career began with the launch of an entrepreneurial design boutique creating a wide range of packaging, publishing, collateral, and advertising solutions for small businesses and large global enterprises. After many years of operating her own business, she built and led in-house digital creative teams for Fortune 500 companies. Over time, her focus shifted from design to the maximization of creative processes, business communications and team dynamics. Being hired by hundreds of companies and hiring hundreds of freelancers, working as employee, contingent worker and entrepreneur, and sustaining a fine art practice in parallel to business ventures, Triandafellos developed insights into the career process. Hearing from college graduates and those exploring career change, she uncovered a large gap in knowledge about how to cultivate a career. *Career X* is Marya's first non-fiction book. Triandafellos has lived her adult life in New York City.

CPSIA information can be obtained
at www.ICGtesting.com
Printed in the USA
BVHW042127010420
576648BV00016B/554